My Art a
Ka

My Art and Skill of Karate

Motobu Chōki

Andreas Quast (ed./transl./pub.)

Motobu Naoki (transl.)

First Printing: 2020

ISBN: 979-8601364751

Andreas Quast (pub.)

76337 Waldbronn, Baden-Württemberg, Germany

www.ryukyu-bugei.com

"Now, when your weapons are dulled, your armor damped, your strength exhausted and your treasure spent, other chieftains will spring up to take advantage of your extremity. Then no man, however wise, will be able to avert the consequences that must ensue.

Thus, though we have heard of stupid haste in war, cleverness has never been seen associated with long delays."

Sunzi Bingfa. Chapter 2: Waging War.

The motto of Baron Oī

SHŌBU

RESPECT FOR MARTIAL VALOR AND SKILLS

Motto brushed by his Excellency Ōi Shigemoto, Member of the House of Lords, Baron, ranked Second Junior Court Rank, former General of the Army, Recipient of the Grand Cordon of The Order of the Sacred Treasure, The Grand Cordon of the Order of the Rising Sun, and The Order of the Golden Kite.

Karate as seen from the medical point of view

Recently, in terms of health care, the motto "prevention rather than medical treatment" is being advocated as the most reasonable thing. Based on this motto, and if you want to prevent illness completely, you certainly ought to strengthen your body so that it becomes more resistant to disease.

There are many ways to promote and preserve health. Among these, the most important thing with the most significant influence on bringing about a healthy and robust physique is the physical exercise of the muscles. This is because it promotes the development of the musculoskeletal system and strengthens the physical basis of the person in its entirety.

It is a crucial matter and a challenging task to select and carefully examine which is the most suitable among the various exercise methods in existence today. However, to summarize this, I think it is essential to precisely determine which is better: to move trunk and extremities together evenly or to develop only some parts of muscles. That is, only when the development of the musculoskeletal system of the whole body is in balance, it can be called a healthy physique. If physical exercise was biased towards only a part of the muscles, the person might lose her physiological balance, and as a result, there is the risk of change towards a deformed physique.

Based on the principles of exercise physiology as described above, and having contrasted it with my knowledge about the improvement of physical constitution as well as the promotion of metabolism, and besides having taken into account its encouragement of *bushidō*, I don't hesitate to affirm that none of the various other training methods currently fashionable is superior to *karate*, which is the most excellent and ideal thing.

Let alone, it prepares proper postures and a majestic appearance, and it is easy to practice. These are, in fact, features that other exercising methods fall short of. Still more, cultivating courage is one of the beneficial points that adds even more splendor to the advantages (of *karate*). For me, the merit of *karate* is not limited to only being a means of physical conflict. Besides, I also won't limit it to being practiced in only one country. By using it (*karate*) exclusively to improve physical education, by expanding and popularizing *karate* not only to the people of All-Japan, but to all men and women of the whole world, and by developing it globally, I hope that we will finally be able to supplement the current deficiencies in the promotion and preservation of health and to reverse the (global trend of) decay in physical constitution.

Right at this time, I have heard that expert Motobu Chōki, who mastered the secrets of this art, will publish a book titled *My Art and Skill of Karate*, in which its techniques are explained. I wholeheartedly support this publication and recommend this book for the sake of the nation. Also, as regards this book project, I do not doubt that it finds favor among the persons concerned with this field of study in the whole country/world. As

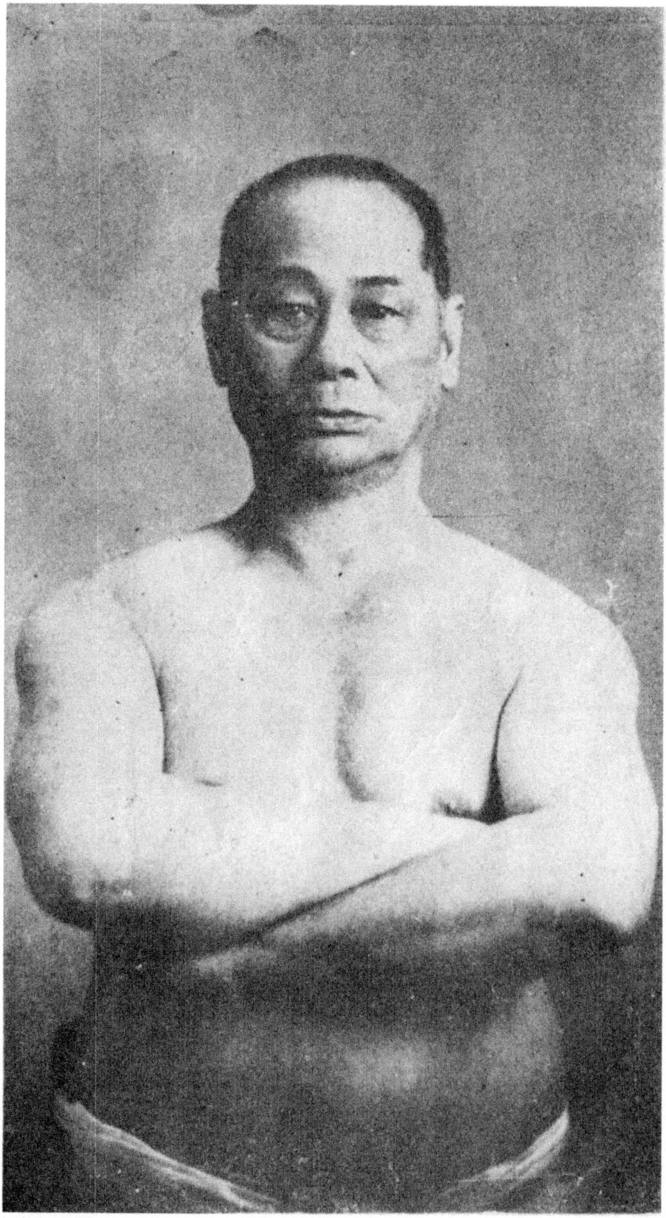

The author, Motobu Chōki (at age sixty-three)

for me, I hope that *karate*, which has a long history, will contribute not only to the world of physical training, but will go even further to have a profound effect on moral and physical education,[1] too. For this reason, I wrote the above thoughts as a brief introduction.

February 20, 1932

Toguchi Seikō, Doctor of Medicine

---

[1] *seishin kyōiku* 精神教育, moral education, in the sense of education that aims to cultivate moral character and the will to practice.

Foreword

THE WAVES OF THE times are considerably rough. The daily lives of both those who live as idealists and those who live as realists are equivalent to struggle. Energetic, spirited, and pure life is being advocated. This purpose requires a strong will, courage, and a healthy body.

Precisely this is the raison d'être of *karate*.

There is no need to explain the expectations set on (this publication by) Motobu Chōki *Sensei*, who is the authority in this field.

Hearing that his book will soon be published, I am beside myself with joy and delight.

Through this book, many like-minded people worldwide will understand the significance of *karate*, and this understanding entirely pushes forward the wheels of history to build a bright, righteous world. I can't stop hoping for people to join together for the spread of *karate*.

March 9, 1932

Sugiyama Kenji, President of the
Waseda University Karate Research Society

Preface

ONCE, IN THE SPRING of 1926, I published a small book to promote the art and skill of *karate.*[2] Just a few years later, thanks to the understanding of well-informed persons and the unremitting efforts of dear researchers and students of *karate*,[3] there is a sudden boom in the study of *karate*, which is now practiced nationwide. This is a great fortune for *karate*.

Also, recently, due to difficulties in social life, young and adolescent students became lethargic, and fell into literary effeminacy without learning physical things, or their speech and behavior became extremely radical. This is indeed a matter of regret. Therefore, in such a situation, it is essential to foster a true martial spirit[4] and to cultivate simplicity and courage.[5] This is the reason why the encouragement of *bushidō* is so prevalent in society these days.

Even though there are already two or three good books (about *karate*), and although I have only superficial academic knowledge, the reason why I present this writing here is that I would like to show the essence of the art and skill of *karate* and to spur this favorable momentum further. It will be my greatest

---

[2] I.e., Motobu Chōki: *Okinawa Kenpō Karate-jutsu Kumite-hen*, 1926.

[3] Refers to specialists and researchers, such as Ōtsuka Hironori, Konishi Yasuhiro, or Yamada Tatsuo. Ōtsuka and Konishi were already specialists in other martial arts, such as *jūjutsu* and *kendō*, and they were interested in *karate*, then an unknown martial art. They learned, studied, and researched *karate*.

[4] *shōbu seishin* 尚武精神, a martial spirit or ethos; a warlike spirit.

[5] *shitsujitsu gōken* 質実剛健. Simplicity and strength; unaffected and sincere, with fortitude and vigor.

privilege if it wins the approval of the general public and many accomplished persons.

I want to express my sincere gratitude to Mr. Kanna Chōjō, who provided significant consideration and assistance in publishing this book, and particularly to his Excellency Baron Ōi Shigemoto, General of the Army, for writing the title motto, and to Dr. Toguchi Seikō and Professor Sugiyama Kenji for their introductions.

March 1932, Tōkyō Koishikawa

The author

Contents

My Art and Skill of Karate

By Motobu Chōki

Karate: Origin and significance

In Ryūkyū, that is, Okinawa, there is a kind of miraculous martial art widely spread throughout the prefecture since ancient times. It is not boxing, and it is not *jūjutsu*, but, while similar to those, it is *karate*, which follows its own distinctive conditions and has a different taste. It is empty-handed and – without carrying weapons – uses the three methods of thrusting (*tsuku*), striking (*utsu*), and kicking (*keru*) to skillfully crush the enemy with one blow, to skillfully suppress brutality with one kick, and it is a martial art entirely made for self-protection that ensures living in peace, and survival.

It was Okinawa, the country of *karate*, that astonished Napoleon, the greatest hero of his era, as a small oriental country that had no weapons.

There are all kinds of theories as regards since what time approximately this miraculous, supreme art and skill of *karate* existed in Okinawa, but, since no clear reference is found in literature, this matter remains unclear.

As regards the source of *karate*, Bodhidharma,[6] the 27th generation successor of Gautama Buddha,[7] came from India to the country of Liang in China. Due to

[6] *Daruma taishi* 達磨太子.

[7] *Shakyamuni* 釋尊, honorific title of Gautama Buddha.

disagreement with Emperor Wu, Bodhidharma left and arrived in the kingdom of Wei in China, where he entered the Shaolin Temple. There he established the theory of "realizing one's nature and making a strong and healthy body."[8] In this way, he devised the original idea of instructing his juniors in both spiritual and physical training. This practice was handed down from generation to generation, combined with the ancient martial arts of China, and became the Shaolin Temple school of *kenpō*, a unique branch of *kenpō* distinguished from other schools. This Shaolin Temple school of *kenpō* entered Ryūkyū. However, following the *Keichō* era (1596-1615), the Shimazu House implemented a political measure of military prohibition, i.e., a ban of martial arts. Therefore, within the specific circumstances of Okinawa, Shaolin *kenpō* merged with native Ryūkyūan martial arts, and as a result of selection and refinement over time, it seems to have developed into *karate*.

[8] *kenshō kyōshin* 見性強身. Basically, this means meditation in combination with physical practice.

Lineages of karate in Ryūkyū

SINCE ANCIENT TIMES, *karate* handed down in Ryūkyū can be broadly divided into the three lineages of Shuri, Naha, and Tomari. However, this doesn't mean that their way of doing things is different. It means that due to the physical constitution of the practitioners and other reasons, the methods of each of the instructors are different, and this has long been a tradition that has been handed down until today.

Since ancient times, in Shuri, at the initial stage of practice, it was made a principle to practice with 60% of the maximum power, and with the single-minded purpose of speed.[9] In Naha, on the other hand, the focus was on 100% maximum power, and it placed emphasis almost exclusively on the development of physical strength. As regards Tomari, it is different from both Shuri and Naha and has been handed down via a somewhat strange lineage.[10]

Until before the abolition of the Ryūkyū kingdom (between 1872 and 1879), because Tomari was Ryūkyū's second trading harbor, frequently ships from countries with which Ryūkyū had friendly relations, such as China

---

[9] Agility, spryness; quickness, legerity, lissomeness; rapidity. See also: On divine speed, page 189.

[10] An original, peculiar, unconventional lineage. Motobu Chōki probably wanted to say that the original teachers of *Tomari-te* were castaways and that *Tomari-te* blends several unique elements.

and Korea, were brought there when they drifted ashore. For this reason, a lodging was established at that place to accommodate the groups of persons who drifted ashore, where, by order of the King of Ryūkyū, these people were warmly welcomed. Therefore, over many years, the villagers of Tomari regularly visited that lodging and received instruction in *karate* from the warriors (*bujin*) who were part of those groups of castaways. This is how Tomari's unique martial art of weaponless self-defense (*kenpō*) was born. However, without understanding the above circumstances, later generations developed a theory about it, misrepresenting it as a Chinese or foreign school[11] handed down in Ryūkyū, and spread its basics posture quite different from the original. In all cases, the correct basic posture is to stand in the character-8-stance (*hachimonji*),[12] and the method of how to employ strength, and of how to manage the feet, etc. are always the same and there is not the slightest difference between them. All of them[13] have their advantages and disadvantages, but it is crucial for the practitioner to purpose speed.[14]

---

[11] For example, because it did not fit into the then fashionable but fundamentally problematic two-sided theory of *Shōrin-ryū* and *Shōrei-ryū*.

[12] i.e. stance in the shape of the character 8, or *hachi* 八.

[13] This refers to the three lineages of Shuri, Naha, and Tomari.

[14] See also: On divine speed, page 189.

The kata of karate, and their transformation

As regards the kata of *karate*, there are too many to name. Some of them fell into oblivion, and some of them are not currently in use, and their rise and fall, and their developments are incredibly complex. Because of this, and along with the changes in the ways of the world, there are two kinds of *kata* in *karate*: *Kata* that are popular, and *kata* that are unpopular. Therefore, I have a feeling that the state of distribution (of *kata*) in Ryūkyū today naturally differs (from previous times).[15] First of all, (*kata* that were) practiced in Ryūkyū since ancient times are Sanchin, Gojūshiho, Sēsan, Sēyunchin, Sūpārinpē, Naihanchi (three levels), Passai (Dai and Shō), Chintō, Chintē, Wanshū, Rōhai, and Kūsankū.[16]

---

[15] I.e., the popular *kata* in the 1800s, 1850s, 1900s etc. may have been different.

[16] Sanchin, Sēsan, Sēyunchin, Naihanchi, Passai, Chintō, Chintē, Wanshū, and Rōhai are written in the *katakana* syllabary. Therefore, the pronunciation reproduced here is true to the original. Gojūshiho, Sūpārinpē, and Kūsankū are written in *kanji*. In case of Kūsankū, the pronunciation is added in *hiragana* syllabary, so it is also true to the original. In case of Sūpārinpē, one *kanji* has *hiragana* syllabary added, according to which the pronunciation would be Ipyaku Rei Hachi. We choose to write it as Sūpārinpē here anyway, simply because it is more widely known. In case of Gojūshiho, no phonetic pronunciation key is added. In the postwar era, an Okinawan *karate* practitioner said that Gojūshiho was once referred to as Ūsēshī in China. However, there is no document nor any other proof for this. Quite on the contrary: In his work *Karate Kenkyū* (1934), Tōyama Kanken added the phonetic pronunciation key *Gojūshiho* to the *kanji*. Moreover, at the primary,

Generally, the three *kata* practiced most widely were Naihanchi, Passai, and Kūsankū.

Moreover, Ryūkyū *kenpō*, or otherwise *karate*, has been introduced from China since ancient times. I guess that Sanchin, Gojūshiho, Sēsan, Sēyunchin, and Sūpārinpē are also often prevalent in China, and currently still exist.[17] Naihanchi, Passai, Chintō, Chintē, Wanshū, Rōhai, and Kūsankū today cannot be seen in their birthplace of China, but are prevalent only in Okinawa. Furthermore, prior to the abolition of the Ryūkyū kingdom (between 1872 and 1879) the two *kata* Wanshū and Rōhai were only practiced in Tomari village, while no one practiced them in Shuri or Naha. Following the establishment of Okinawa prefecture (in 1879), Wanshū and Rōhai also came to be frequently taught in Shuri and Naha. Pinan was devised by the early modern warrior (*bujin*) Itosu *Sensei* to be used as teaching material for his students, and as a genuinely unique *kenpō* of Okinawa, it is a great fortune for this field of study.

---

middle, and normal schools in Shuri, were *karate* was taught by Itosu, Yabu, and Hanashiro from around 1905, only the standard Japanese language was allowed, while dialect was strictly prohibited. Therefore, we tentatively transcribed it here as Gojūshiho.

[17] This was written long before the cultural revolution in China, so it is possible to a certain degree.

A short instruction on kenpō

A. Practicing *karate*: Beginning the initial stage of practice at the age of twelve has the advantage that one can develop significantly, and also that one becomes trained thoroughly and systematically. However, as long as you are determined, you can begin practice at whatever age you like. If possible, it is best for both one's physique and one's technique to practice continuously throughout one's whole life.

B. Those who aspire to practice *karate*, or those who already practice it, always also devote time and energy to their weak side, and during the time of practice, they keep in mind to use their left hand a lot. Even when practicing twice during morning and evening, you must always exercise to improve the strength of your left hand as much as possible.

C. Those who want to practice *karate*, and also those who endeavor to train martial arts, in general, must make an effort to develop both of their hands physically. Always when getting up, while sitting on the mattress, place much strength in the center of your body[18] and move both hands together two or three times

[18] *tanden* 丹田, point about 3 cm below the navel, considered the center of the body; a focus point for internal meditative techniques.

alternately up and down, or back and forth, or left and right.

D. If you practice *karate*, always bear in mind that its basic stance is the character-8-stance (*hachimonji*). Also, not only during times of practice but habitually, you should throw out your chest and place much strength into your lower abdomen (*tanden*) so that you don't relax your posture. Those who have practiced *karate* for a long time all have a better physical constitution and a more robust health than ordinary people. Whenever they practice, they throw out their chest and place much strength in the lower abdomen (*tanden*). As a result, they never lose their posture, and it has become habitual, and gradually the body becomes trained well so that it reacts immediately, and since the body becomes stronger more and more, practice should never be neglected.

E. Among the practitioners of *karate*, some often argue that the room is too small for practice, but this is a severe indiscretion. Anyone who has the correct spirit called *bu* (martial), because you can practice under any circumstances, you have to try to practice without fail, twice a day in the morning and evening, even if it is only in the corner of a room. Also, you must try to practice regularly, because it is a necessary condition for the practitioner in sense of reviewing the material already learned.

F. It would be severe misbehavior if a *karate* practitioner would behave hot-blooded in youthful ardor,[19] or if he would not solely use it to defend himself, but would abuse *karate* to bully the weak. The practitioner always bears in mind, and complies with the correct meaning of *bu* (martial) and, in the spirit of modesty and self-discipline, must never forget the concept of *bu* at any time.

G. *Karate*, being a quite valuable and universal martial art, is also a resource for mental training, that is, the cultivation of the mind. Those who practiced *karate* developed a strong unity of mind and body, became immovable,[20] and never lost their composure. In these points, the practice of *karate* coincides with that of *zen*.

---

[19] I.e., to act indiscriminately on a temporary passion.

[20] Never get perturbed or agitated; never get anxious or get excited; never feel nervous.

How to clench a fist (tējikun)

JUST AS THE BASIC *karate* stance since ancient times has been determined to be the character-8-stance (*hachimonji*), the Ryūkyūan way of clenching the fist also follows a prescribed manner.[21]

First, let me tell you about the sequence of gripping:

Stretch out straight the first four fingers (i.e., index finger, middle finger, ring finger, and little finger); grasp your fingers profoundly as you gradually fold them starting from the fingertips; at the same time, bend your thumb, place it above both your index and middle fingers, and put strength into it.

The image (on page 13) shows the outer and inner side of the clenched fist.

[21] *Tējikun*, phonetically more precisely pronounced *tījikun* in Okinawan dialect, has the meaning of a 'clenched fist' (*kenkotsu* 拳骨) or 'fist' (*kobushi* 拳) in the Japanese language.

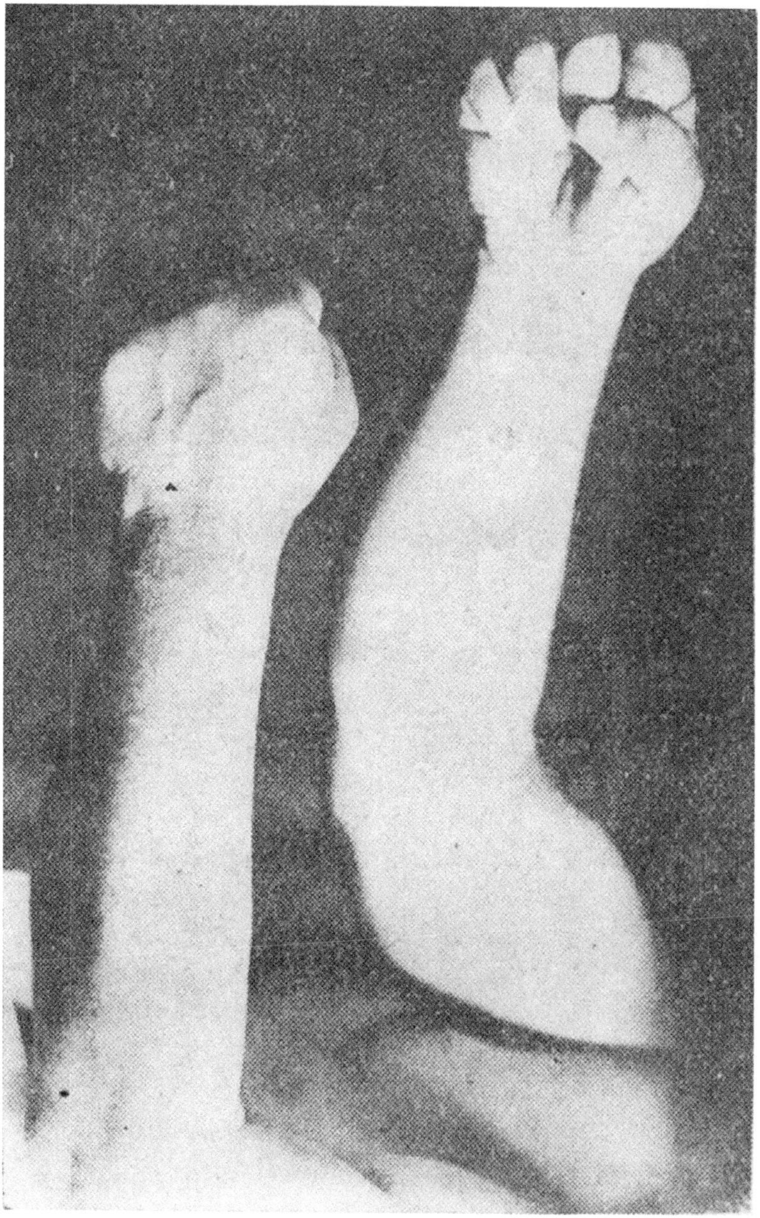

The standardized form of the coupled hands (meoto-de)

IN CASE OF ACTUAL COMBAT, both hands must always be positioned as shown in the previous image (on page 13). This position is usually referred to as 'coupled hands' (*meoto-de*). [22] Speaking of how to make practical use of these two coupled hands, since the front hand fights in the front line, it both attacks and defends. In other words, whether it thrusts, or whether it receives the enemy's attack, it immediately thrusts at the same time. The rear hand is continuously employed as a reserve, so when you can't make it with your front hand, you can still attack and defend with your rear hand. As to how to assume this hand position, this seems to be usually unknown. Often, when other *karate* practitioners establish their hand position, only one hand is placed forward, while the other hand is attached to the side of the torso, in preparation to thrust.[23] And those *karate* practitioners call the forward hand a defense, or dead hand, and call the rear hand an attack, or live hand. But this kind of hand position is a severe mistake, and

---

[22] *meoto-de* 夫婦手 means 'coupled hands', a descriptive term which perfectly illustrates the intended meaning both literally as well as metaphorically.

[23] This refers to the position called *hiki-te*, or *pulled-back hand*, which has become a trademark of modern *karate*, and which still recently spurred all kinds of explanation attempts to make tactical sense of it.

incompatible in case of actual combat. With this kind of hand position, there is the risk of being too late in a real fight. It is advantageous that the attacking hand is as close to the enemy as possible, so that as a result quick actions can be performed. When you see this hand position practically applied in *kumite*, you will realize its high effectiveness.

How to clench the one-knuckle-fist (ippon-ken, kōsā)

IN RYŪKYŪ, SINCE ANCIENT times the way of how to grip the one-knuckle-fist (*ippon-ken*)[24] became habitual without words of explanation. How the one-knuckle-fist (*ippon-ken*) is clenched in accordance with a specific rule, and as is often done since childhood, is shown in the photo (on page 17).

First, bend the middle finger, ring finger, and little finger, all three at the same time. Next, raise out the index finger higher, and then apply pressure to the side of your index fingertip with your thumb, and particularly place strength in your thumb and index finger. Also, when clenching the *ippon-ken,* it is optional to either use the index finger or the middle finger.[25] However, judging from my experiments, rather than using the grip shown in the following image (page 17), I think that it is more effective to strike with the two knuckles of both index finger and middle finger.[26]

---

[24] *ippon-ken* 一本拳, or one-knuckle-fist. The proximal interphalangeal joint of the index finger. Today it is also known as *shōken*. In the chapter's title, Motobu adds the term *kōsā* コーサー as another old designation for *ippon-ken*. *Kōsā* appears to be one of the very few designations of old-style *karate* techniques that are still currently handed down in Okinawa.

[25] Today often referred to as *nakadaka ippon-ken*.

[26] The *Motobu-ryū* uses both index and middle fingers, so it is actually a *nihon-ken*.

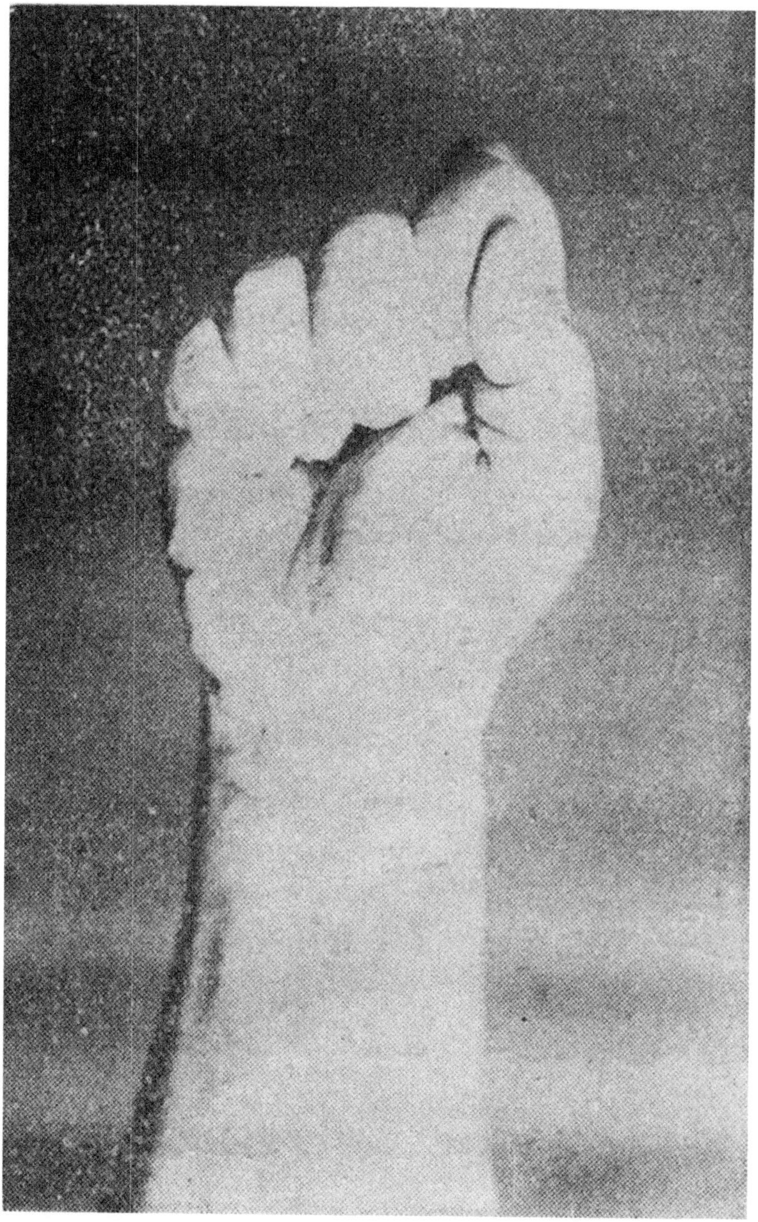

The basic posture, and koshi

WHEN PRACTICING KARATE, YOU should always keep in mind its basic stance and how to put strength in it, that is, how to apply your lumbar region (*koshi*[27]).

As mentioned earlier, the basic stance in any situation is the character-8-stance (*hachimonji-dachi*), i.e., with the tips of the toes opened, pointing outward in the shape of the Japanese character 8. Depending on the person, there are slight differences in the distance between the feet, but about 45.45 cm would be a good reference value. In addition, you should always keep in mind how to apply power, i.e., how to use your lumbar region (*koshi*) and how to put strength in your lower abdomen. This standard form derives from the natural way of human walking, and the stance while striking the *makiwara* as well as the stance of Naihanchi (see image 3 of Naihanchi Shodan, page 45) are also done in the character-8-stance.

---

[27] *koshi* 腰: Refers to the abdominal segment of the torso, between the diaphragm and the sacrum and includes the lower back, the waist, and the hips.

How to construct a makiwara, and its method of practice

AMONG THE INDISPENSABLE EQUIPMENT of *karate* practitioners is a practice tool called *makiwara*.[28] Intended to be instrumental in the training of the fist, when you have trained with it for several months, your fist is well capable of crushing several roof tiles and wooden boards with a single blow.

There are two types of *makiwara*: the hanging *makiwara*,[29] and the standing *makiwara*.[30] Usually, the standing *makiwara* is simply referred to as *makiwara* and is used by many people. Other than the standing *makiwara*, the hanging *makiwara* is used less often, and only by a few people.

I will now give a detailed explanation of how to construct a *makiwara*:

For the hanging *makiwara*, place about 30 kg of sand in about ten bundles of straw. The length should be between around 45.45 cm and 120 cm. Next, wrap it

[28] *makiwara* 巻藁, literally 'straw wrap', refers to a wooden post wrapped with straw as a surface to practice impact techniques such as thrusts, strikes, and kicks.

[29] *sage-makiwara* 提巻藁.

[30] *tachi-makiwara* 立巻藁.

tightly with a rope. Hang it from both ends with a rope and thrust it while it hangs down.[31]

For the standing *makiwara*, start by making flat straw cords, which you then wrap around straw, thus creating a so-called *makiwara* or straw wrap that is about 30.3 cm long and 10.6 cm wide. Tie this to the wooden post and thrust against it (see image 1, page 23).

Generally, the dimensions of the wooden post are as follows:

- Overall length: 212 cm (136 cm above ground, 76 cm below ground)
- Width: 10.6 cm
- Thickness: upper end 1.5 cm, lower end 7.2 cm

There is another training tool that is also simply called *makiwara*. It is a variety of the standing *makiwara* and mainly intended to contribute to the development of both arms. Although this variety is not generally used, it should be detailed here for reference. This kind of *makiwara* is made from a round wooden post with a diameter of about 9.2 cm and a length of 212 cm. Of this, a ratio of about 136 cm is above ground, and 76 cm is below ground. It is buried in such a way that it doesn't move in the ground. With a thickness of not less than 3 cm and over a length of approximately 30 cm straw cord is tightly wrapped around it. Strike it with

[31] Like a sand bag, just hung horizontally. There is a picture of such a hanging *makiwara* on page 112 of Mabuni Kenwa's book *Kōbō Jizai Goshin Kenpō Karate-dō Nyūmon* 攻防自在護身拳法 空手道入門, 1938.

both forearms from the front or the side. This contributes to the development of muscles and bones.

Furthermore, as regards how to thrust a *makiwara*, stretch out the chest as much as possible, stand in the form of character-8 (*hachimonji*), and thrust alternately with the left and the right hand. First, practice standing with the right foot forward and strike with the left hand (see image 1, page 23) and with the right hand (see image 2, page 25). Next, repeat the same practice as before, this time with the left foot forward, as shown in image 3 (page 27).

It should be noted here that when practicing on the *makiwara*, when the thrusting hand moves with 80% power, the power of the hand pulling back should always be 100%, and you should start practicing with the left hand. The reason why is that, in whatever person, the left hand is still inferior in strength to the right. Therefore, I think you should continuously practice in the morning and the evening, and in such a manner that if the right strikes 20 times, the left strikes 30 times, and if the right strikes 30 times, the left strikes 40 times.

Also, as shown in image 4 (page 29), stand at the side of the *makiwara* and practice strikes with the side of the hand (both on the right and left).

Also, as shown in image 5 (page 31), practice the foot, that is, kick with the part of the foot that is between the toes and the plantar arch (i.e., the ball of the foot).

The hanging *makiwara* is mainly used for practicing the foot, and don't forget to practice all three: the heels, the part between the plantar arch and the toes, and the toe tips. However, since a hanging *makiwara* is designed to move up and down, since the olden days, it also contributed to the development of muscles and bones by thrusting or otherwise striking with your feet, hands, or the back of the elbows.

Explanation: How to strike the makiwara

As shown in image 1 (see page 23), stand with your right foot forward, in the form of character-8 (*hachimonji*), and apply your hips (i.e., the lumbar region, or *koshi*).

Start (to strike) with your left fist first.

At the outset, hold your left fist on the side of the torso, as shown in image 2 (see page 25), and then thrust.

Along the trajectory, twist your arm inwards (clockwise) so that the back of the hand faces upwards. Fully extend (the arm) and strike with the four knuckles of the index and middle finger (i.e., the metacarpophalangeal joints and the proximal interphalangeal joints, and over the length of the proximal phalanges).

When pulling back (the other hand), pull your elbow back as far as possible and with plenty of power.

And, the amount of power used is 80% when thrusting, and 100% when pulling back.

Image 2 (see page 25) shows how to thrust with the right hand. All else is the same as in the previous description.

Image 3 (see page 27): Stand with the left foot forward and strike. All else is the same as in the previous descriptions.

However, right-handed people should thrust twice as often with the left hand than with the right. Furthermore, as you gradually become more proficient, you should practice thrusting left and right alternately.

As shown in image 4 (see page 29), stand at the side of the *makiwara*, in character-8-stance (*hachimonji-dachi*), and apply your hips (*koshi*), and practice striking with the side of the fist.

And do not forget to practice this with both the right and the left hand.

As shown in image 5 (see page 31), when striking with your foot, you should fully stretch out your leg.

Practice equipment

GENERALLY, THERE ARE SPECIFIC exercising tools for all types of physical exercise, although their shapes vary in accordance with the nature of the exercise. In the same way, there are also practice tools indispensable for the practice of *karate*. Many of them are still the same practice tools as used in primitive times. While in today's civilization some people reject them, precisely these primitive utensils are essential for the practice of *karate*.

First of all, there is an oval-shaped stone of about 42 kg. It is necessary for the beginner as an indispensable item to increase physical strength. That is, the practitioner lifts it twice a day, every morning and evening. It is a necessary item to measure one's increase in strength. From there, together with your gradual increase in strength, you should try to use oval-shaped stones of up to about 78 kg.

Furthermore, there are the *chīshī* (mounted stone, *sueishi*) and the *sāshī* (stone shackle; stone lock) that can be used to increase the physical strength of both arms.

The *chīshī* is made of a round, disk-shaped stone or iron, in the center of which a wooden handle is inserted with a length of about 30.30 cm to 36 cm to 40 cm. Held at the end of the handle, the *chīshī* can be stretched out and extended in all directions.

The *sāshī* is shaped like a lock and made of stone. It is loaded on the back of the hand and also practiced to increase the physical strength of both arms by extending it back and forth and left and right. Depending on the person's arm strength, its weight varies, but generally, each of them weighs approximately 6 kg.

Understanding practice – The story of the venerable gentlemen Matsumura, Nagahama, and Itosu

THERE IS THE OFTEN-HEARD expression *warrior of great strength*,[32] but it seems that its method and principles differ greatly depending on the teacher. Since this is such an essential matter, and since there still seem to be people who misunderstand it, I would like to explain it, particularly for those who are going to practice *karate* in the future. As an example of it, I would like to introduce an episode in which Nagahama *Sensei* from Naha praised Matsumura *Sensei* from Shuri Yamagawa.

Matsumura *Sensei* was a little older than Nagahama *Sensei*. With his martial qualities being of considerable scope, Matsumura *Sensei* was by no means a warrior (*bushi*) who flaunted only his strength.[33] And Matsumura *Sensei* always remained calm, and determinedly monitored the enemy's movements, and was able to apply techniques freely.

---

[32] *chikara bushi* 力武士.

[33] For example, like a macho. It means that Matsumura *Sensei* was clever and not only knew about muscle strength, but also about speed, timing, as well as the importance of appreciation of other people etc.

For a long time, I have also received regular instruction from Matsumura *Sensei*, and the practice of *kata* always focused on how to place power into *kata*, as well as on the practical use of *kata*. That's true just like that, and I have been following his teachings to this day. Even if your strength is superior to that of other persons, and your body is well trained: If you have not fully mastered the practical applications, in a sudden situation you will be unable to act with speed, and because of this, such a martial art (*bu*) is of no use whatsoever.

By the way, when talking about the kind of person Itosu *Sensei* was, with both his physique and martial strength, he was undoubtedly an outstanding warrior (*bujin*). When my elder brother (Motobu Chōyū) practiced martial arts, because Itosu *Sensei* would come to our house every day, I practiced together (with my elder brother Chōyū and Itosu *Sensei*) since I had been about twelve or thirteen years of age. But since I was bullied by my elder brother every time, I've been continuously thinking about how I could win against him. In the end, since practicing with Itosu *Sensei* alone wasn't enough, and I was not satisfied with it, I went to study under Sakuma *Sensei* from Gibo and Matsumura *Sensei* (from Yamakawa). I secretly went back and forth and studied various things, and from the age of about twenty years, I was confident that I could gain victory against my brother. Nevertheless, I still visited Itosu *Sensei* at times and received various commentaries (on my technique). Then, after Itosu *Sensei* had come to appreciate (my ability in *karate*), he revealed to me the following story about the last request by Nagahama *Sensei*, which was unknown to me.

Originally, Itosu *Sensei* first received instruction from Matsumura *Sensei*, but because Itosu *Sensei* was sluggish, Matsumura *Sensei* disliked him. Therefore, although he practiced enthusiastically, since his teacher was essentially negligent towards him, Itosu finally retired and decided to attend Nagahama *Sensei* of Naha.

While Nagahama and Itosu differed only one year in age,[34] they did form a master-and-student relationship. Nagahama *Sensei* was a well-known person at that time. Having a quite ardent zeal, he was always out in the garden early in the morning, started to practice, and it seems that he stopped only when the evening sun went down in the west, and his practicing shadow would reach his wife's weaving loom.

But it seems that Nagahama *Sensei* strongly opposed Matsumura *Sensei* and devoted all his power to strengthen his body when practicing. When Nagahama *Sensei* faced his death, he called his leading disciple, Itosu *Sensei*, to his bedside, telling him his last request:

> "As for me, up to now, I have practiced as hard as I could, but did not at all think about the actual situation (of fighting), and I lack freedom and agility (of movement). Since I thoroughly realized this point today, from now on, please study under Matsumura."

You should take this to heart.

[34] Nagahama was one year older.

In repeating myself: In practice, if you understand its principles and if you practice the basics (*kihon*, i.e., *kata*), the muscles become naturally trained and considerably strong. But if you do not thoroughly understand what is called practical application and speed, everything else is worthless.

The kata Naihanchi, and misinformation about it

IN NAIHANCHI, AND I think you already know this, the feet are opened in the character-8-stance (see image 3 of Naihanchi Shodan, page 45). When standing in the character-8-stance, these days, it is generally taught to squeeze the soles of the feet together and to apply strength to tighten (the muscles of) the insides (of the legs), and people also believe that this is legitimate, but it is extremely misleading. This form is used exclusively by those who follow the tradition of the venerable Itosu. From the venerable Matsumura and the venerable Sakuma, I've been taught in such a way to generate strength by merely opening the feet into the shape of the character-8-stance (*hachimonji*). Since, at first, this point was also quite doubtful to me, I asked both the venerable Matsumura and the venerable Sakuma about it.

The venerable Matsumura's statement was:

> "When used in an actual fight, Itosu's small-turtle-form of standing is extremely dangerous. One would immediately be overthrown!"

After having considered this carefully, I want to follow the venerable Matsumura's opinion. First, if you try to stand in the character-8-stance (*hachimonji*) of the Itosu school,[35] and squeeze the soles of your feet together, and another person just slightly pushes you from behind with the fingertips, you will easily fall over. Thus, no matter how much strength is put into this posture, there is no effect whatsoever. *Kata* should be taught as close as possible to its use in reality (i.e., actual combat), and not selectively to increase strength (i.e., for physical training purposes). For this reason, I can't admire leaving behind to future generations a *kata* far removed from reality. Because of that, I cannot approve of squeezing the soles of the feet together, and at the same time, I dare to reveal this mistake to a broad public.

---

[35] Motobu here actually refers to it as *Itosu-ryū*. In the above quote on page 38, Matsumura called this way of standing "Itosu's small-turtle-form," or *kamigwa-gata* 亀小型.

Naihanchi Shodan

NAIHANCHI IN TOTAL CONSISTS of thirty-three behavioral patterns. [36] For your convenience, a few commands have been added to each to illustrate the sequence of movements.

IMAGE 1*

The posture of preparation (*yōi*).

Place strength into your lower abdomen, straighten yourself and look to the front.

This posture puts strength into your whole body and demonstrates your will for self-protection.

* *The corresponding images are always on the opposite, odd-numbered page.*

---

[36] Motobu Chōki presents thirty-four images with description, but image 1 and image 34 are considered the same position. Therefore the sum of behavioral patterns becomes thirty-three.

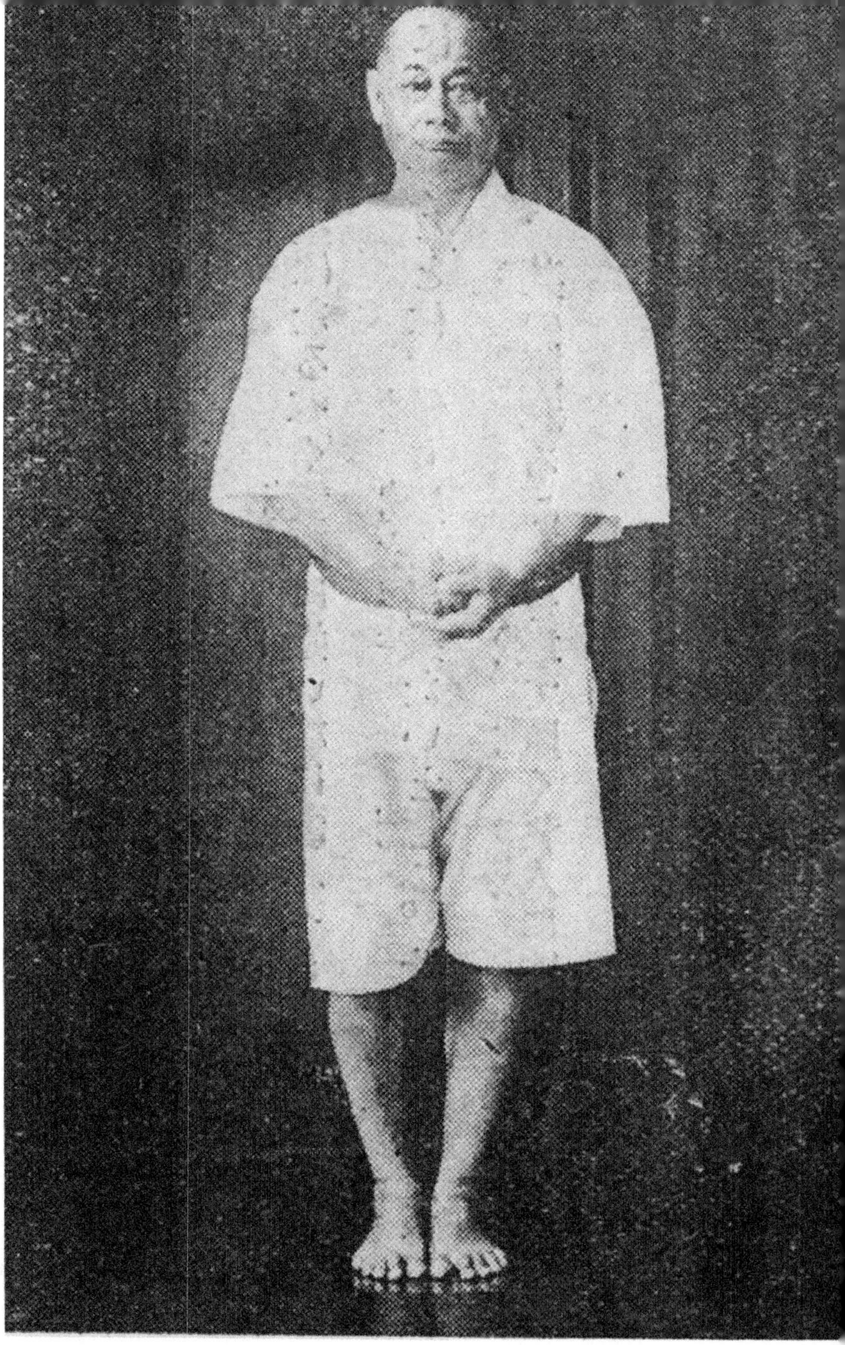

IMAGE 2

As you look to your right side, simultaneously cross your left foot slightly over your right foot, as is shown in the image (on page 43). Note that as soon as you're being attacked from the right side, step in with one step and receive (defend) it, and simultaneously commence combat.

IMAGE 3

From the second command, extend your right hand to the right side and, at the same time, step to the right with your right foot, as is shown in the image (on page 45). And while clenching your left fist, thoroughly pull it back to the left side of your torso, and do not let your upper body posture collapse, but place strength into your lumbar region (*koshi*), and with the legs as if riding a horse, with a feeling as if tightening the force of both legs from the outside towards the inside, stand firmly with a sense of actively tightening your strength, and notice the transition from the previously described (cross-legged) stance to the character-8-stance (*hachimonji*). The distance between the feet should be about 45.45 cm. The eyes look straight into the face of the enemy. At the time the right hand is stretched out and strikes, it simultaneously receives (defends) the enemy's attack. And thus, because it has the meaning of seizing the enemy's hand (arm, forearm), you should turn your palm (vertically). Also, it should be understood that stepping forward (from cross-legged to character-8-stance) includes the meaning of kicking the enemy.

IMAGE 4

From the third command, as if grabbing something with your extended (right) hand and pulling it towards yourself, strike the enemy with your left elbow, as shown in the image (on page 47). However, at that moment, with the elbow about 15.15 cm from your chest and your upper body facing to the right, you should be careful that the lower part of your body does not collapse.

Note that in actual combat, you should not strike with your left elbow, but thrust with your left fist. Precisely because this is *kata*, it has to look good, and so that it conceals (the real combat applications). This is important to note.

IMAGE 5

From the fourth command, place both your fists on top of one another at the right side of your trunk, with the left fist on top (and palm facing downward, and the right fist at the bottom, with the palm facing upward), and at the same time look to the left side.

However, at that moment, you should straighten the posture of your body and be careful not to raise your left shoulder.

This posture is to turn towards the left side and prepare yourself to attack.

IMAGE 6

From the fifth command, without letting your previous posture collapse, strike down your left hand as it is (to a position) in front of your kneecap.

If you assume that the enemy tries to knock you down with a kick of his foot, the meaning is to knock (sweep) aside his foot.

IMAGE 7

From the sixth command, twist up your left hand (to the left side of your torso) and simultaneously thrust out the right hand, as shown in the image (on page 53), (so that it is) above (the left hand).

However, note that the right arm gradually lowers from the shoulder to the fist, as if water flows down over it. And note that the distance between the arm and the chest is about 15.15 cm.

This type of move means to thrust the enemy who is near at your side.

IMAGE 8

From the seventh command, with your previous posture as it is and without letting it collapse, cross your right foot slightly over your left foot.

Note that this is a preparation for advancing sideways.

IMAGE 9

From the eighth command, while opening your left foot one step to the left, raise your right arm, as shown in the image (on page 57), and look to the front again.

The distance between your (right) fist and your face should be about 30 cm, and the distance between your (left) armpit and (left) elbow should be approximately 15.15 cm.

The movement of stepping forward has the (hidden) meaning of knocking down the enemy at your side with a kick.

IMAGE 10

From the ninth command, the right hand knocks down, and simultaneously the left hand knocks up in front of the right hand as if the tips of the hands are drawing circles, resulting in the posture as shown in image 10 (see page 59).

While doing so, you should value doing it as fast as possible. Note that *kumite* image 9 is an application (*ōyō*) of this form of movement (see page 129).

In this form of movement, when the enemy is coming in (with an attack), you knock it down with your right forearm.

IMAGE 11

From the tenth command, without letting your posture collapse, strike with your left fist, as if striking in the face of an enemy in front of you, and while thoroughly doing so, have your left elbow placed on your right wrist.

IMAGE 12

From the eleventh command, look to the left side and, as shown in the image (on page 63), simultaneously sweep the front with your left foot. Return your foot to its original position. This return action has the (hidden) meaning of kicking the enemy who is in front.

IMAGE 13

From the twelfth command, twist the upper body to the left and receive (defend) a strike that is coming from the left side.

At the time of this move, some people teach you to twist your forearms quite a bit, and this is greatly erroneous, too, because this is not a method of defense with the palm of the hand. You should pay attention to this.

IMAGE 14

From the thirteenth command, look to your right side and, at the same time, as is done in image 12 (with the left foot, see page 63), sweep the front with your right foot and then return your foot to its original position.

This foot sweep has the (hidden) meaning of kicking the enemy who is in front.

IMAGE 15

From the fourteenth command, as shown in the image (on page 69), twist your upper body to the right and receive a strike coming from your right side, and use your right arm to protect yourself.

Image 16

From the fifteenth command, as is shown in the image (on page 71), place fist upon fist on the right side of your body, with the left fist on top, and simultaneously look to your right side. Be careful not to raise your shoulders.

This is the preparation for the next move.

IMAGE 17

From the sixteenth command, push out both your hands on top of each other to the left side, without losing your posture.

Its meaning is to receive (defend against) a thrust coming from the enemy. This movement is an application of the so-called 'coupled hands' (*meoto-de*).

IMAGE 18

From the seventeenth command, thoroughly pull your right hand back to the right side of your torso, and simultaneously, while twisting it up, open your left hand, as shown in the image (on page 75).

You should do this to seize the enemy with your left hand.

IMAGE 19

From the eighteenth command, twist your upper body to the left and simultaneously strike with your right elbow, as shown in the image (on page 77). However, take care not to let the lower part of your body collapse.

IMAGE 20

From the nineteenth command, while looking to the front, join both your hands on the left side of your torso, as shown in the image (on page 79).

IMAGE 21

From the twentieth command, look to the right side and simultaneously strike down your right hand, as shown in the image (on page 81).

IMAGE 22

From the twenty-first command, link your hands on the right side of your torso, as shown in the image (on page 83).

Image 23

From the twenty-second command, without letting your posture collapse, in preparation for moving to the right, cross your left foot slightly over your right foot.

IMAGE 24

From the twenty-third command, advance your right foot one step to the right. The distance between feet is about 45.45 cm to 60.6 cm.

IMAGE 25

From the twenty-fourth command, look to the front and raise your left hand, as shown in the image (on page 89). Note that your (left) fist is slightly below eye-level and approximately about 45.45 cm in front of the shoulder. The intention should be to intercept attacks from the front.

IMAGE 26

From the twenty-fifth command, from in front of your right shoulder, strike down your left hand. Simultaneously, shoot up your right hand starting from the outside of your left shoulder, with quick movements, and assume the posture shown in the image (on page 91).

IMAGE 27

From the twenty-sixth command, while positioning the left arm (about horizontally) in front of the body, and supporting the right elbow as shown in the image (on page 93), hammer out your right forearm to the front, and (immediately) return it to its original position.

IMAGE 28

From the twenty-seventh command, while looking to the right side, and while not letting your posture collapse, sweep as if you kick up to the front with your right foot, as shown in the image (on page 95), and return the foot to its original position (on the floor).

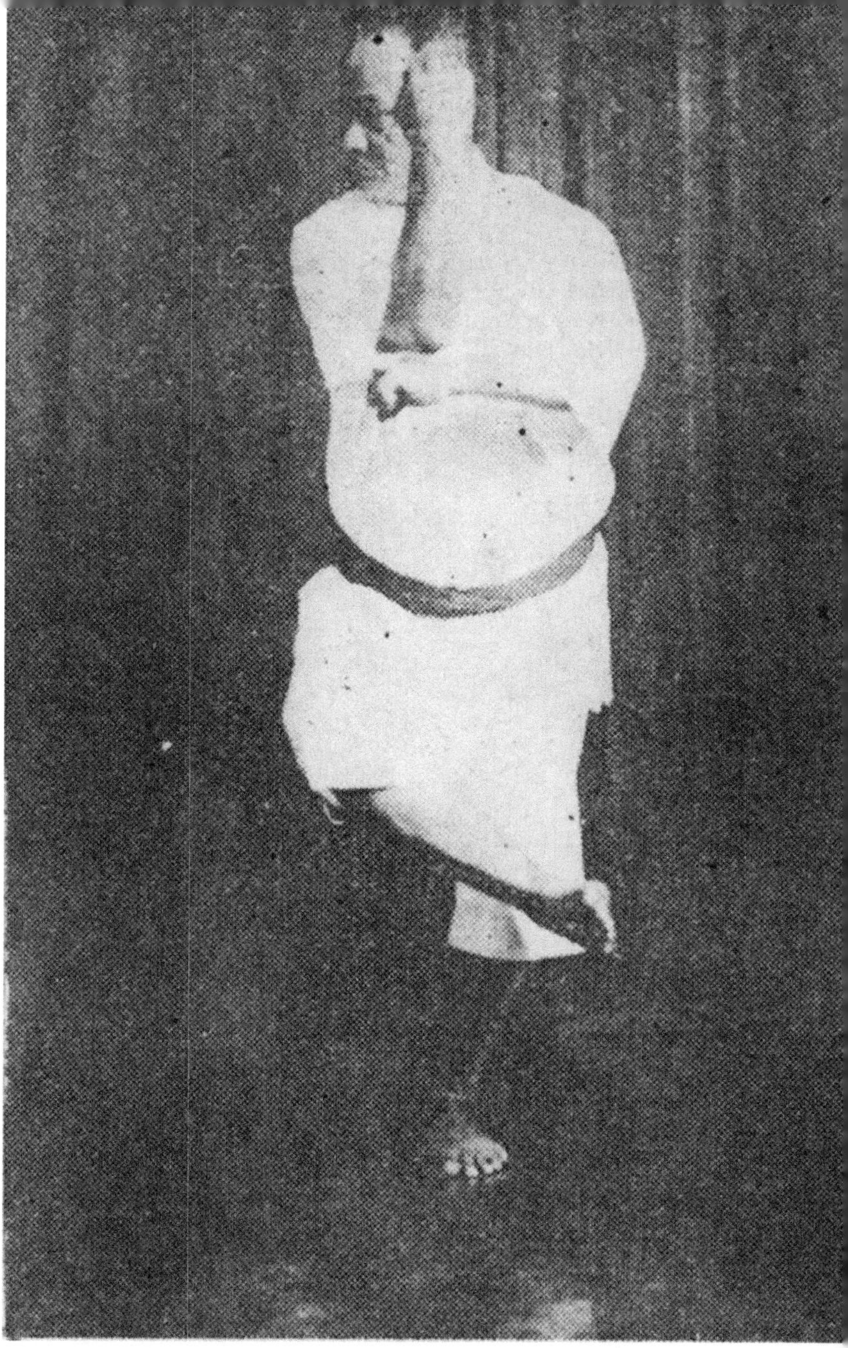

Image 29

From the twenty-eighth command, without collapsing the posture of your lower body, twist your upper body to the right and receive an attack coming from the right side (as is shown in the image on page 97).

IMAGE 30

From the twenty-ninth command, look to the left side, and sweep as if you kick up to the front with your left foot, and return the foot to its original position (on the floor).

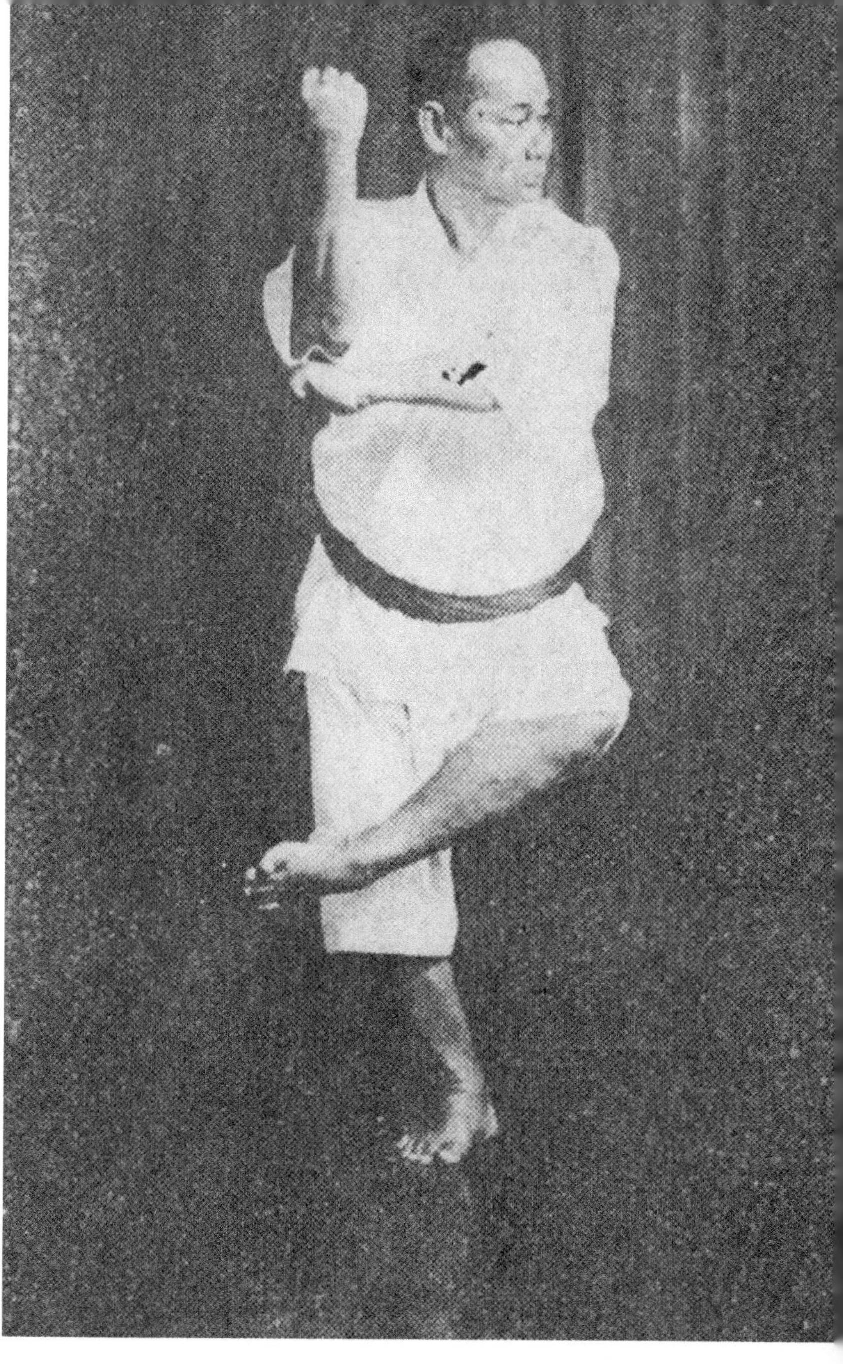

IMAGE 31

From the thirtieth command, turn your upper body to the left side together with your arms, as shown in the image (on page 101), so that you can receive (defend) an attack coming from the left side.

IMAGE 32

From the thirty-first command, while looking to the front, place your arms on the left side of your torso, as shown in the image (on page 103).

IMAGE 33

From the thirty-second command, look to the right side and thrust out both your left and right hands.

IMAGE 34

From the thirty-third command, pull your right foot (to your left foot), and simultaneously look to the front and pull both hands back to return to the first position (of the *kata*).

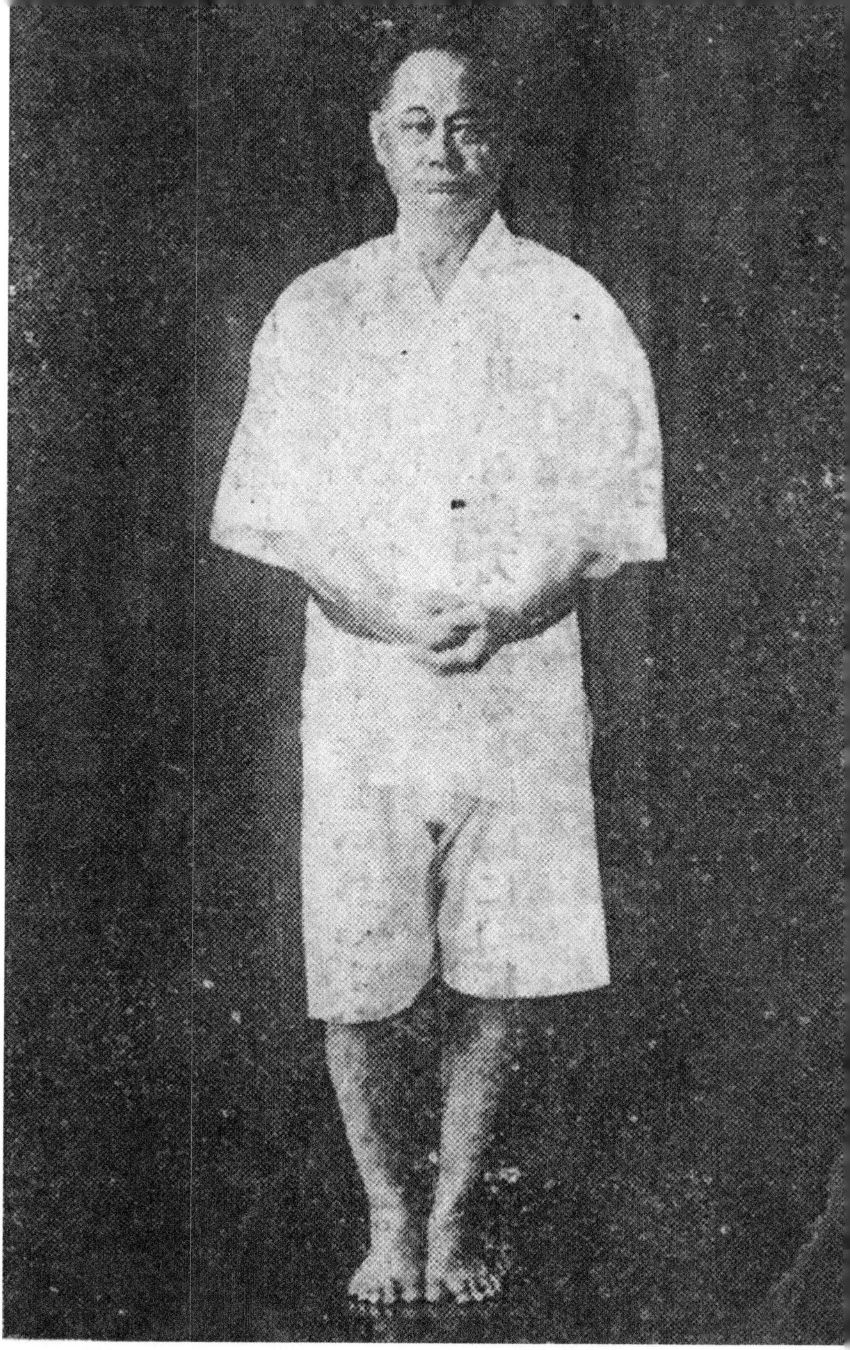

Understanding posture (kamae)

There are various types of what is usually called posture (*kamae*), but I want you to know that these are just outer forms. Nevertheless, it should not be neglected at all. In the case of real combat, if a person says you should always adopt the posture like this or like that, I would object and say that there is no fixed outer form in postures (*kamae*). I argue that this is because posture (*kamae*) is a state of mind (and not a mere physical, outer form). It is always important to be prepared to deal with the requirements of the moment, that is, in case of being attacked in an instant situation. Therefore, it should not categorically be said that "this posture is good" or "that posture is good" (judging only from its outer appearance). In short, you should pay attention to the fact that posture (*kamae*) is a matter of training your martial strengths every day, and coincident with it, to train your mind and spirit.

Karate ni sente nashi

THERE IS THE EXPRESSION called *karate ni sente nashi*, which some people interpret in its literal sense (as "there is no first move in *karate*"), and some people seem to frequently teach it as "you must not move (=attack) first," which I think is quite a misunderstanding. Indeed, the thing called martial spirit[37] is never practiced to beat up other people without reason. I think you already know that training the mind and body must be the primary purpose.

Therefore, this expression means that you should not cause harm indiscriminately, and if you are forced to, that is, when it is unavoidable, and the enemy tries to harm you, you must stand up and fight ferociously. When entering a fight, it is essential to dominate the enemy, and to dominate the enemy, you must move (attack) first. Therefore, when entering a fight, you must move (attack) first. This is important to keep in mind.

[37] *shōbu seishin* 尚武精神, the correct spirit of respect for martial valor and skills.

Kumite

RYŪKYŪ KENPŌ KARATE CAN be divided into basics (*kihon*) and *kumite*. Because *kihon* is the foundation of *karate*, it is commonly referred to as *kata* (such as *Naihanchi*, *Passai*, etc.), and it is frequently taught to beginners, too.[38] *Kumite* is somewhat like *Kime-no-kata* of *jūdō*, but in contrast to *Kime-no-kata, kumite* it is done consecutively, section by section, as a whole.[39] In the Ryūkyū language, the term *kumite* seems to be a corruption of "to cross or to link the forearms with one another," or "to grapple with the forearms."[40] However, it should be noted that while *kumite* has been carried out in Ryūkyū since ancient times, there is still no standardized *kata* of *kumite*. Also, nothing about it has been left behind in literature. There are also so-called reference books for *kumite*,[41] but since many of them were compiled by Chinese martial artists, and were then valued and copied by (Okinawan) martial artists, a characteristic Ryūkyūan *kumite* has not yet been compiled. By its very nature,

---

38 This means, *kihon* = *kata*, and *kata* = *kihon*.

39 This means that the techniques and combinations are not individually itemized, as in case of *Kime-no-kata*, but done consecutively along the series of movements of the *kata*.

40 *te o kumu* 手を組む. *Te* 手 in Japanese has two meanings, namely 1. the hand, and 2. the arm from elbow to the fingers. Here, *te* 手 is meant as in 2. The verb *kumu* 組む here means 1. to cross; to link; to intertwine; to enwine. 2. to bind together; to tie; to connect; to join. 3. to wrestle; to grapple; to struggle; to compete.

41 This most probably points to the *Bubishi* or *Bubishi*-like documents.

karate is a strong and courageous martial art. Therefore, even among those whose technique is still inadequate, some pose a threat (to others by *karate* technique). Generally, only those who have graduated from basic training (i.e., *kata* such as Naihanchi, Passai etc.) are ready to experiment and practice receptions (*uke*) and releases (*hazusu*)[42] with each other. Because of this, there are all sorts of variations depending on the person, and there are no standardized *kata* of *kumite*. That being the case, those who attempt to practice *kumite* should always choose opponents suitable to them, and who understand that in *kumite* agility and speed is the most important thing.[43] And when you frequently practice receptions (*uke*) and releases (*hazusu*) with the right partner, because you will then have sufficiently practiced *kumite*, you can expect your skills to improve naturally. This seems to be the most important thing.

---

[42] *uke hazusu* 受けはづす. In accordance with a given tactical context, this refers to either or a combination of 1. techniques such as escaping from holds of the wrist, the lapel, clothes, body, choke-holds and the like. 2. techniques that divert an attack; to dodge; to evade; to avoid; to sidestep; to ward off; to move out of the way.

[43] See also: On divine speed, page 189.

IMAGE 1*

When the opponent grabs you by the collar with his right hand, seize the opponent's wrist from below with your left hand. When (then) the opponent thrusts to your face (with his left hand), slightly squat and enter deeply,[44] while simultaneously blocking with your right arm upwards.

* *The corresponding images are always on the opposite, odd-numbered page.*

---

[44] The expression "enter deeply" should be understood as in *irimi* 入身 or entering into the opponent's posture. As a consequence, the position of the block is not at the opponent's wrist, but further up the forearm, such as shortly before the opponent's elbow or further up the arm. The *Motobu-ryū* blocks higher up the arm, not close to the wrist.

IMAGE 2

If you (then) firmly pull the opponent's wrist as shown in image 2 (on page 115), and simultaneously thrust the opponent below the chest with your right fist, you win.

The same is done when he grabs you by the collar with his left hand.[45]

* *This is a continuation of number 1.*

[45] It means, you can do it just the same on the either side.

IMAGE 3

As before, when the opponent grabs you by the collar with his right hand, seize the opponent's wrist from below with your left hand. Simultaneously, seize his right arm (above the elbow) with your right hand, and firmly pull him towards yourself.

* *This is an alternative continuation of number 1.*

IMAGE 4

As shown in the image (on page 119), stretch the fingers of your right hand and use your sword hand (*shutō*) to strike the opponent's side of the torso.

It is the same as when he grabs you by the collar with his left hand. (winning technique[46])

* *This is another alternative continuation of number 1.*

[46] *kachi-de* 勝手. It is unclear why this term was added here, and only here. It is not a Japanese composite word. The same expression was used in the *Bubishi*, also to mean "winning technique" and contrasted by a "loosing technique." Anyway, in Motobu Chōki's book this expression appears only once. Maybe it was used in Okinawa in olden times, but we dont know for sure.

IMAGE 5

As in the previous image, when grabbed by the collar, seize your opponent's wrist with your right hand, and slightly dodge your body away (clockwise).

* *Number 5 is the same situation as in number 1, but with the other side of the body.*

IMAGE 6

With the opponent in this very disadvantageous position, vigorously pull the opponent's right hand towards yourself, and at the same time, with your left fist, thrust him in the chest as shown (in the image on page 123).

* *This is a continuation of number 5.*

IMAGE 7

The opponent is still steadfast and thrusts with his left fist. At that time, thoroughly pull his (right) wrist towards yourself and enter with your left hand (forearm) as shown in the image (on page 125). Press down the opponent's left arm and pull your left and right arms with a feeling as if drawing a bow.

* *This is a continuation of number 6, in case the technique was unsuccessful.*

IMAGE 8

When the opponent thrusts to your face with his left fist, enter deeply[47] and block with your arm (sideways), and like this receive (*uke*) and release (*hazusu*)[48] as shown in the image (on page 127). At that time, hold your left hand attached to the right forearm as a reserve.

* *Here starts a new technique, showing how to use the coupled hands (meoto-de) in kumite.*

[47] The expression "enter deeply" should be understood as in *irimi* 入身 or entering into the opponent's posture.

[48] *uke hazusu* 受けはづす. In accordance with a given tactical context, this refers to either or a combination of 1. techniques such as escaping from holds of the wrist, the lapel, clothes, body, choke-holds and the like. 2. techniques that divert an attack; to dodge; to evade; to avoid; to sidestep; to ward off; to move out of the way.

IMAGE 9

When the opponent still thrusts with his right hand, receive it by knocking it down with your right hand, and strike the opponent's face with your left fist.

* *This is a continuation of number 8.*

IMAGE 10

Mutually cross your right hands (forearms). When you have assumed this posture, the opponent strikes to your flank with his left fist (as shown in the image on page 131).

* *Here starts a new technique.*

IMAGE 11

At that time (when he thrusts), slightly change (twist) your upper body and receive it (with your right arm) as shown (in the image on page 133). When he (then) thrusts with his right fist, receive it with your left hand (forearm) from the inside (*uchi-uke*). However, if (on the outset) your left hand is not always attached to your right forearm as a reserve, it is impossible to receive (defend against) it.

* *This is a continuation of number 10.*

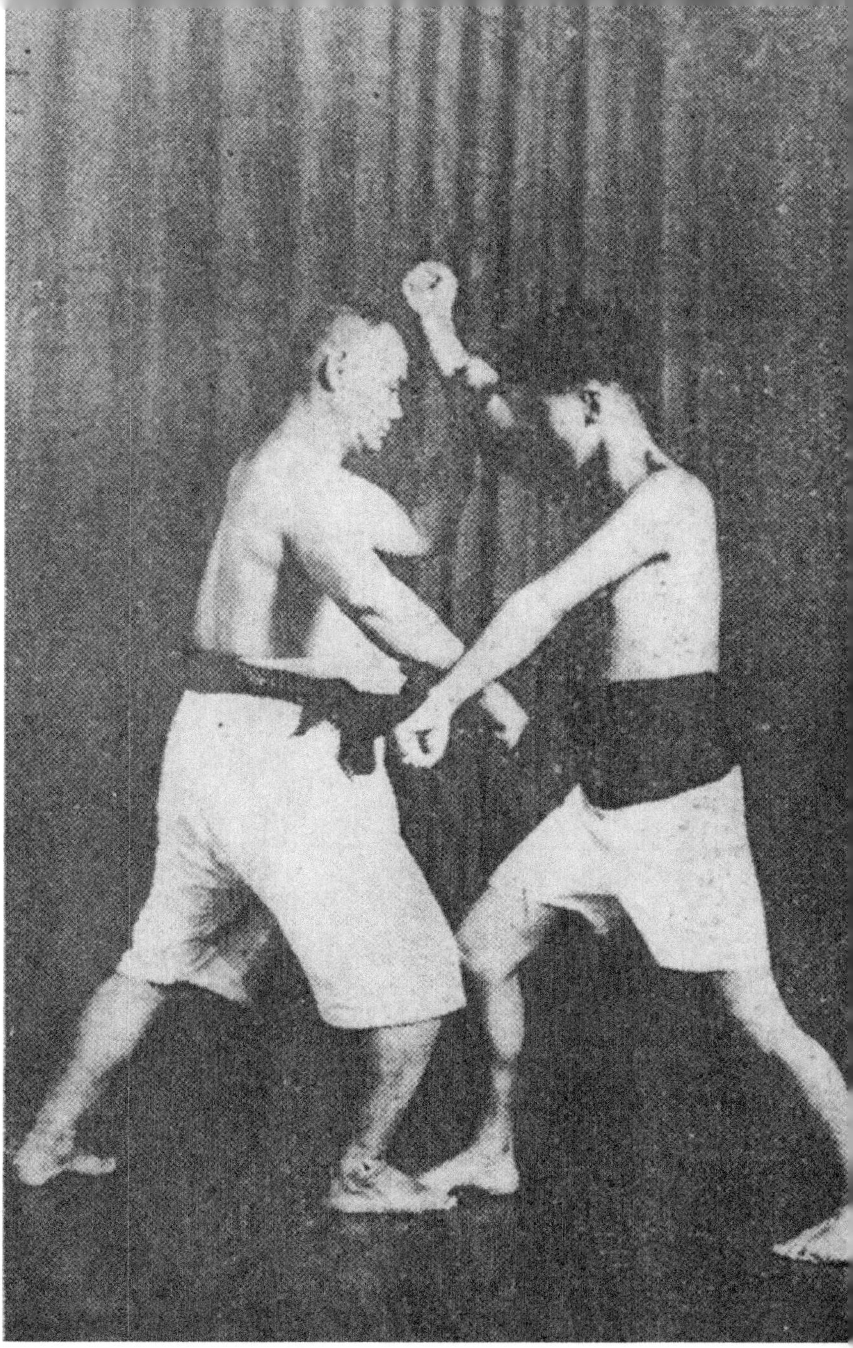

Image 12

As soon as you received it, immediately take hold of both his arms as shown in the image (on page 135), and strike the opponent's testicles with your (right) knee.

* *This might be a continuation of number 11.*

IMAGE 13

When the opponent thrusts (with his right hand), when you receive it (with your left hand), immediately seize his wrist and raise it, and step into him with your right foot and seize his testicles with your right hand.

* *Here starts a new technique.*

IMAGE 14

When you have seized his (right) wrist (with your left hand) and raise it, step into him with your right foot and, at the same time, strike his chest with your (right) elbow, as is shown in the image (on page 139).

* *This is an alternative continuation of number 13.*

IMAGE 15

When he thrusts towards your face (with his right hand), dodge your upper body to the opponent's right side, receive his thrust on the outside (*soto-uke*), and thrust the opponent's side of the torso (with your left fist).

* *This is the same attack as in number 13 but with a different counter.*

IMAGE 16

When the opponent thrusts with his left fist, change (twist) your upper body, and receive his thrust from the outside (*soto-uke*) with your left arm (forearm). And if he still kicks with the left foot (leg), receive it by knocking it down, with your left hand, and thrust the opponent's flank with the right hand.

IMAGE 17

When your right hands (forearms) mutually cross each other's, and the opponent thrusts with his right fist,[49]

* *Here starts a new technique.*

[49] The photo shows the right forearms connected. But the opponent holds his left fist in front. This must be ignored here: in fact, in the following step he thrusts with the right hand. The left hand is of no interest here. While this is a little confusing, consider the opponent's posture as also being in *meoto-de*.

IMAGE 18

(then) swiftly twist your upper body (to the right) and with your left hand (forearm) receive your opponent's right hand (arm) from the outside, and because this creates an opening, you should thrust his chest immediately (as is shown in the image on page 147).

* *This is a continuation of number 17.*

Image 19

You are unexpectedly seized from behind (with both arms around the chest and above both arms).

* *Here starts a new technique.*

Image 20

Apply force as you spread out both your arms (to make space), lower your body weight (*koshi*) a little, and rotate your hand as shown in the image (on page 151) to seize his testicles.

* *This is a continuation of number 19.*

Martial artists of Ryūkyū, and their unique skills

ALTHOUGH THE *KENPŌ KARATE* of Ryūkyū is something traditional, there is no literature in its home country about when it was begun to be practiced widely, and there are no historical sources about it that could be researched.

For this reason, I will here introduce a series of biographies of martial artists which I have heard from older people, and these are only martial artists since the last three hundred years.

When listed in chronological order, in Shuri there were Nishinda *Uēkata* (aka Sabi no *Uēkata*), Sōryo Tsūshin, Gushikawa *Uēkata*, Tokashiki *Pēchin*, *Tōdī* Sakugawa, Ginowan *Dunchi*, Makabe *Chān*, Ukuda, Matsumoto, *Bō* Miyazato from Teshiraji, and 'Guan Yu' Sadoyama.

Later in the period there were Tsuken *Hanta-gwā*, Chatan Yara, Ōta *Aji*, Ōta Nagasutarū, Uehara, Matsumura, Ishimine from Akahira, Hokama, Motomura, Sakihara, Andaya Yamagusuku, Tōma *Pēchin*, Nomura, *Bō* Nagusuku, Shichiyanaka *Usumē*, and Ishimine from Samukawa.

In more recent times there were persons such as Ufugusuku, Kanagusuku, Tawada, Tomigusuku *Uēkata*, Tamagusuku *Uēkata*, Sakuma, Kyan, Kunjan

[Kunigami], Suishi [Soeishi] *Uēkata*, Makishi, Itosu, Asato, and Gima the *Chikusaji.*

In Naha, there were persons such as Gushi, Sakiyama, Nagahama, and Kuwae. All these were well-known martial artists (in Naha).

In addition to the above, there were experts of *tsukite (chichidī)* such as Matsumora, Oyadomari, and Yamada as three persons from Tomari, Murayama from Kume, *Bō* Kohagura from Gusukuma village, and Miyahira from Kohagura village.

Moreover, there was 'wholesale,' that is, there were countless self-proclaimed experts of *karate.*

Now I will introduce each person and their special skills (not strictly in chronological order and not all persons):

Nishinda *Uēkata* was commonly called Sabi no *Uēkata.* He was the ancestor of today's Nishinda (Nishihira) in Shuri Gibo. It is said that, in addition to *karate*, he was also skilled with the *yari* (spear).

Gushikawa *Uēkata*, simultaneously with being an expert of *karate*, was a swordsman of Ryūkyū of that time and a master of the wooden sword (*bokutō*).

Sōryo Tsūshin, a martial artist of the same era as Nishinda *Uēkata* three hundred years ago, accumulated the hard practice of this art, to which he devoted himself. Although he was a monk by profession, he is said to have been one of the best among the martial artists of Ryūkyū at that time. Moreover, he also excelled in all kinds of other martial arts (*bujutsu*), and reportedly his abilities were such that he overwhelmed others.

Tokashiki *Pēchin* is said to have been known as the greatest eccentric of Ryūkyū. He was known for his eccentricity rather than for being a martial artist. He was also skilled in humorous poems, and he is said to have crushed sake bottles with one single strike of the palm of his hand.

Tōdī Sakugawa is a person who drew a line in terms of martial arts (*budō*) when comparing it with [the martial arts of] the previous era of Ryūkyū. After him, there was no-one like him (i.e., he remained unequaled). As a man admired among martial artists still in posterity, there was no man superior to him in terms of ability and other things. Moreover, as is well known, he was a master of the 'triangle jump' (*sankaku tobi*): when matched against another person, by a technique so fast that the eyes could not follow, he 'kicked up' triangular walls without slackening at all, and completely sangfroid, which is indeed formidable.

Tsuken *Hanta-gwā* and Shichiyanaka *Usumē* were known as masters of the *bō.*

Ginowan *Dunchi*, the father of famous Giwan Chōho, stood at more than 191 cm and weighed more than 138 kg. He was remembered by the people of that time as a huge man and as a possessor of superhuman strength. He distinguished himself in the technique of knocking down/shooting down a swallow with a palanquin carrying *bō* with a diameter of 6.7 cm and a length of more than 2.12 m. When Ginowan was kneeling, an adult person was able to hide completely behind him.

Makabe *Chān* stood at a body height of 160.6 cm and – with a corpulent physique – he looked bovine at first sight. Notwithstanding, because he trained in the martial arts, and as his nickname *Chān-gwā* ('the rooster') accurately indicates, he was very nimble and bounced around in all directions as if he was a rooster. In fact, at the residence of the Makabe *Udun*, which had remained unchanged since those days, on the ceiling of the reception room of that residence one can still see the trace of his foot from the time when he oiled his sole, jumped up, and kicked the ceiling. Seeing this footprint, one will agree as to how exceptionally nimble and skilled he was with jumping techniques.

'Guan Yu' Sadoyama, as his name implies, was the owner of a beautiful beard. He was said to have resembled Guan Yu of old China, who indeed looked like Sadoyama. He is said to have been skilled in *karate* and in addition to having been a master of the *yari* (spear).

Uehara was a master of the *sai*.

Motomura was widely known as a master of the *bō*. He was also called an archetypal giant and majestic man. When he seized a six-foot wooden staff (*rokushaku-bō*) facing the enemy, it was as if there were no enemies on any side. For example, he bored holes into both walls of the room. The tips of the *bō* barely fitted into these holes. Then, standing in the center of the room, he threw the *bō* to the left and right, always thrusting into the aforementioned holes with one hundred percent marksmanship, and he seemed to have failed not even once.

Sakihara and Hokama were two persons of the same era. Both of them were known as persons of unparalleled herculean strength. Particularly Hokama, who, together with Matsumura, received instruction in swordsmanship (*kenjutsu*) from Ijūin of Satsuma, was an expert of striking with the [probably wooden] sword.

Ukuda and Matsumoto were known as experts of *tsukite (chichidī)*.

Ōta *Aji*, together with his younger brother Nagasutarū, were not only known to possess herculean strength, but also as martial artists who have both wisdom and courage.

Ishimine from Akahira was also known to possess herculean strength.

In addition to the above, the martial artists (*bushi*) known by name in those days were:

Andaya Yamagusuku, although the public didn't particularly know him, he was a person who is said to have gone to China on purpose and studied *karate* and also distinguished himself in archery.

Matsumura, Tōma, and Nomura were all martial artists of the same era. The people knew Matsumura *Sensei* as a man of unparalleled bravery. He was from the Bu-clan, his Chinese-style name was Seitatsu and his pen name was Unyū. He freely handled his footwork and was excellent at kicking upwards.

Occasionally, when a comrade tried to restrain him by throwing his arms around him from behind, although Matsumura *Sensei* could not use his hands, he freely kicked up with his legs on the left and the right. In this way, he kicked down the person who threw his arms around him from behind. And he was also a swordsman. According to one theory, to take retribution on his uncle's enemy, he went to China on purpose to study *karate*, and he received instruction in swordsmanship (*kenjutsu*) from famous swordsman Ijūin from Satsuma, whose secrets of swordsmanship Matsumura *Sensei* mastered. Besides being skilled in martial arts, he was also a prodigy of that era. He became an authoritative calligrapher (*shoka*) and skillful painter of literati painting (*bunjinga*). Since around twenty years of age, he became a personal attendant (*sobayaku*) of King Shō Kō. The king liked pranks, so Matsumura once participated in a bullfight match organized by the king.

At that time, there was a famous ferocious bull kept at one of the secondary villas of the king. Because Matsumura *Sensei* anticipated the king's prank, he immediately went to the barn to see the ferocious bull. Upon seeing Matsumura, the bull stamped with its hooves and bristled with anger through the nostrils. *Sensei* first tried to punch it with his clenched fist, but the bull didn't weaken easily. Because the bull butted with his horns more and more violently, Matsumura *Sensei* then attacked it with a folding fan. Every time the bull attacked again, Matsumura *Sensei* punched its eyes with the folding fan. Even a bull like this finally lost its heart. *Sensei* then went to the barn every day and repeated this. From this episode, we can understand the importance of thorough preparation for martial artists. That is, *Sensei* knew the weak point of the bull in advance, and he made the bull realize it, too, and he made the bull fear.

However, the king ordered Matsumura *Sensei* to the bullfight match, and *Sensei* accepted it. Finally, the appointed day has had arrived. The king had a railing constructed around the bullring. Outside of it, the spectators waited in breathless excitement. Pulled with a rope by two persons, the famous ferocious bull entered the ring. When glancing at *Sensei*'s expression, he wore his usual court clothes, and only held a fan in his hand.

Although the king was exceedingly worried, he gave the royal order for Matsumura *Sensei* to wear light clothes, but *Sensei* entered into the railing unblinkingly and without any hesitation, and assuming guard position with nothing but a fan in hand. To tell how the match went, the huge bull came charging three or four times, but every time the beast got scared of *Sensei* to poke his eyes (with the fan). And when *Sensei* advanced, the bull flinched and fled. The audience was completely in awe (surprised) and their appreciation for *Sensei* seemed to increase more and more.

Sensei always used to lecture to us how the work of the intellect is necessary for a thorough preparation of martial artists.

Incidentally, Yabu Kentsū, as a neighbor of Matsumura *Sensei*, was one of those who had been loved very much by *Sensei*.

Tōma *Pēchin*, a man also from the Matsumura period, was an eager researcher of *karate* who outstripped the others in skill.

Nomura was a giant with a body height of over 166.65 cm. With an impressive body, he is said to have been skillful in knocking down a person with a single strike. And since no person was able to withstand his single strike, he is remembered by posterity as the greatest *Tījikun Bushi* of his age.

Ufugusuku and Kanagusuku were both of the same era. Ufugusuku had excellent abilities and devoted himself to the study (of the martial arts). Kanagusuku was strong-muscled. When he straightened himself and clenched his fist, it is said that his body became exactly as firm as a stone.

Chikusaji Gima was unparalleled in terms of ability. Posterity celebrated him as a martial artist skilled with the *sai*.

Ishimine from Samukawa was agile, and his techniques were nimble. Moreover, he was known as a preserver of traditional *karate*.

Furthermore, among the martial artists of the early modern times (since the Meiji era), there was Sakuma the Wise, who is said to have plunged into a water well and supported himself in the air by clamping both legs, and did not fall back in the water. Also, he wrapped a woven straw mat around his body, with nothing but both hands and the head sticking out, and – in one go – broke out from inside the 121.2 cm woven straw mat, which indicates his hard practice.

Kunjan was an enthusiastic researcher with techniques so fast that they are said to have been admired together with Tawada's kicking techniques.

Kyan[50] was a famous person who could make his body hard as iron.

As an early modern era martial artist (since the Meiji era) of the same generation as the venerable elder Itosu, Tomigusuku *Uēkata* was a master of the *Koi-ryū*. At present, his favorite disciple Izena Chōboku is still alive. Tomigusuku also distinguished himself in spearmanship (*sōjutsu*) and it is said that people valued his horsemanship over his *karate*. Particularly, with his specialty being spearmenship on horseback, when Tomigusuku mounted his marvelous 182 cm tall chestnut-colored horse and seized his *yari* (spear), any enemy – how formidable he might have been – flinched.

Tamagusuku *Uēkata* was of the same era as Tomigusuku. Tamagusuku was the leading disciple of Makiya and received the favor of the master. Moreover, as an expert of horsemanship (*jōbajutsu*), Tamagusuku was skilled in the *Shintō-ryū* and also distinguished himself in archery. These two men were celebrated as the two matchless people of horsemanship in Ryūkyū.

Makishi, as a master of 'rope tearing' (*nawagiri*), was skilled at wrapping a rope around his body two or three times and – with a fighting yell (*kiai*) – was able to tear the rope completely. Moreover, he would wrap a *hachimaki* of white cotton cloth around his head very

---

[50] Does this refer to Kyan Chōfu?

firmly, which he then shook off by shaking his head just once.

Both the venerable elder gentlemen Asato and Itosu are more recent martial artists of Shuri. The venerable Asato had a light body and a fast technique, while the venerable Itosu, in an exclusive research attitude, was eager to practice on the *makiwara* all the time. Itosu, as a martial artist of the early modern times (since the Meiji era), was a rarely seen expert of *tsukite (chichidī)*.

Although younger than the two persons mentioned above [Asato and Itosu], there are Kiyuna and Itarashiki from Shuri as two venerable elder gentlemen known as experts of *tsukite (chichidī)*. Itarashiki was known by the nickname Akāyamā. Although he currently is at the old age of eighty-one years,[51] his vigor surpasses that of men in their prime. With a muscular body, and also skilled in horsemanship, he is a holder of sophisticated *karate* skills. He is also an excellent singer of songs from the Yaeyama Islands region (*Yaeyama-bushi*).

As regards the martial artists (*bushi*) in Naha, Gushi was famous during the generation of Uehara from Shuri. Gushi was known for his nimble and fast techniques as well as for his *tsukite (chichidī)*.

Nagahama was a master of *tsukite (chichidī)*. The venerable elder Itosu became his disciple.

Kuwae was a person equally admired as Nagahama and was also from Naha at that time. With a body as hard as iron, he was indeed a giant.

---

[51] So he was born around 1851.

Among the martial artists from Tomari, whatever others may say, the three persons Matsumora, Oyadomari, and Yamada achieved exceptional praise.

Matsumora was a master of *tsukite (chichidī)*. I (=Motobu Chōki) asked him for instruction from time to time. Matsumora *Sensei*'s teaching methodology was to continually have his disciples thoroughly reflect on the best way to do things (as if thinking about a *kōan*). The teaching method of *karate* from Ryūkyū is generally so that the technique of those who do not thoroughly reflect on the best way to do things does not quite progress, and usually, they only succeed in strengthening their bodies.

Oyadomari was an expert in kicking techniques.

Yamada possessed the particular skill of making his body hard, and in this regard, he is equally admired as Kuwae.

As regards other martial artists from Kume village during the Itosu era, there was Murayama, who surpassed the ability of the other people and who was an extraordinarily healthy and vigorous man.

Finally, in finishing this manuscript, I introduce *Bō* Kohagura from Gusukuma village and Miyahira of Kohagura village. Since olden times, martial artists of Ryūkyū did not only practice *karate* all the time (consistently), but everyone also had special skills. These two persons, too, excelled in *bō* and horsemanship. During the time of Matsumura, Kohagura was one of the best *bō* fencers.

Miyahira, too, as a martial artist of the same period, was well known. He made himself a considerable name as an expert of horsemanship and had a hugely built body.

Martial Artists Throughout the Eras

The Era of King Shō Kei (rg. 1713–1751)

- Nishinda *Uēkata* (aka Sabi no *Uēkata*)
- Sōryo Tsūshin
- Gushikawa *Uēkata*

From King Shō Boku (rg. 1752–1794) to King Shō On (rg. 1795–1802)

- *Tōdī* Sakugawa
- Ginowan *Dunchi* (Morishima *Uēkata*)
- Makabe *Chān*
- Ukuda
- Matsumoto (the ancestor of Yabu Kentsū's clan)
- *Bō* Miyazato from Teshiraji
- 'Guan Yu' Sadoyama
- Tokashiki *Pēchin*

From King Shō Sei (rg. 1803) to King Shō Kō (rg. 1804–1834)

- Tsuken *Hanta-gwā*
- Gushi (from Naha)
- Chatan Yara
- Ōta *Ajī*
- Ōta Nagasutarū
- Uehara
- Matsumura
- Ishimine (from Akahira)

- Hokama
- Sakihara
- Andaya Yamagusuku
- Tōma (*Pēchin*)
- Nomura
- *Bō* Nagusuku
- Shichiyanaka *Usumē*
- *Bō* Kohagura
- Miyahira from Kohagura Village
- Ishimine from Samukawa

From King Shō Iku (rg. 1835–1847) to King Shō Tai (rg. 1848–1872)

- Tawada
- Tomigusuku *Uēkata*
- Sakiyama (from Naha)
- Ufugusuku
- Kanagusuku
- Tamagusuku *Uēkata*
- Sakuma
- Kyan[52]
- Kunjan (Kunigami)
- Suishi (Soeishi) *Uēkata*
- Itosu
- Makishi
- Asato
- Nagahama (from Naha)

---

[52] Does this refer to Kyan Chōfu? Kyan is a person from the days when kings Shō Iku and Shō Tai reigned. Since the reign of these two kings lasted from 1835 to 1879, and Kyan Chōfu was born in 1839, he belongs to this era.

- Kuwae (from Naha)
- Matsumora (from Tomari)
- Oyadomari (from Tomari)
- Yamada (from Tomari)

Anecdotes about martial artists of the modern era

The heroic tale of Gushikawa Umikami, the prodigy of this field of expertise

There once was a person from Akahira named Gushikawa Umikami, whose name is remembered by posterity. He was the leading disciple of Nishinda *Uēkata*, who was also known as Sabi no *Uēkata*.[53]

Umikami was originally from the House of Haneji, and his older brother Ungan ('Cloud Rock') is well-known as a celebrated priest of Ryūkyū. Besides, he is also known as the main character of anecdotal stories such as about crushing demons, so his name has been handed down to posterity.

At that time, within the office organization of the royal government of Ryūkyū, there was a duty called *wakashu* ('Young Men Group'). When Umikami was only 13 years old, he served at the royal castle as such a *wakashu*. One day, together with a couple of friends who also served as *wakashu*, Umikami left the castle and made on his way home. When they happened to pass in front of Adan Spring, because he was so thirsty, he

[53] Sabi 左部 is his former territory name. Sometimes, the surname changed with a change of territory.

wanted to drink. Near the river, he noticed a bucket with water and drank from it without permission.

However, a certain manservant of the Nakata *Dunchi*, who had been watching the situation for some time, got angry like a raging fire, and everyone was terrified by his unparalleled herculean strength. Seizing Umikami by the nape of the neck, and not listening to the boy's apologies, and behaving overall ill-mannered, he struck Umikami on the top of the head with his huge clenched fist.

Even though Umikami was not weak, he ran home crying and told the story to his father and Sabi no *Uēkata*. Then, for the shame received from that manservant, in tears, he begged his father, *Uēkata*,[54] to become the disciple of Sabi no *Uēkata*, who was famous at the time.

However, Sabi no *Uēkata*, taking only a quick look at Umikami, saw through the matter and said,

> "This person will become Ryūkyū's greatest martial artist (*bujin*) in the future, and will surely make a name for himself in posterity."

Sabi no *Uēkata* assumed full responsibility (from the father) for instructing Umikami in *karate*.

Within a few years afterward, Umikami became an outstanding warrior. By the time he was 16, he was approved as the leading disciple of his teacher Sabi no

[54] Motobu Chōki mistook this: The Haneji *Udun* were of royal *Aji* or *Ōji* rank, not *Uēkata*. The Haneji *Udun* and the Nakata *Dunchi* were both members of the Oroku *Udun*.

Uēkata. Without even a bit of arrogance and always treating other people with a humble attitude, it is said that he was famous as a prodigy in this field of study.

Particularly, his composed courage has been handed down to posterity in several oral traditions, of which I'd like to give one or two examples. Once, wanting to test his attentiveness as a warrior, Sabi no *Uēkata* called his name through the sliding door. Umikami placidly kneeled at the sliding door, bowed politely, and as a precaution against the sliding door screen being shut abruptly, he took his fan in hand and inserted it in the sliding door groove.

On seeing this, with Umikami being attentive in every situation and despite being only sixteen years old, his teacher Sabi no *Uēkata* highly praised his attitude of never neglecting his composure as a warrior (*bushi*). Furthermore, by the time he was seventeen years old, to wipe out the disgrace he had once received at Adan Spring, Umikami through his teacher (Sabi no *Uēkata*) forwarded the challenge to a duel (held in the presence of a high-ranking personality[55]) to the manservant of unparalleled herculean strength. Finally, both decided to fight for life and death at the Taira horse-riding ground within the next few days.

One day within the next few days, Umikami was snoring loud while taking a nap in his small four-and-a-half-mat room. Just then, the teacher Sabi no *Uēkata*

---

[55] *gozen jiai* 御前試合, literally this refers to a competition in the presence of the emperor, the *shōgun*, a *daimyō*, or in this case, the king or a similarly high-ranking personality. This is because Umikami was also a member of the royal class.

came to visit Umikami and saw him sleeping fearlessly in his room. In the presence of the father, Sabi no *Uēkata* grabbed a six-foot staff (*rokushaku bō*) and chopped away with it at Umikami. Even though he was supposed to be sleeping, Umikami jumped up and while remaining completely calm, he warded off the staff strikes of his teacher with one of the *tatami* mats stacked up around him.

In this way, within just a few years of receiving moral and physical influence and guidance by Sabi no *Uēkata*, Umikami became Ryūkyū's most celebrated warrior (*bujin*). At the duel (held in the presence of the king or a similarly high-ranking personality) at the Taira horse-riding ground, Umikami knocked down the manservant of unparalleled herculean strength with one blow. His name is widely-known to posterity.

Tokashiki Pēchin, who was rich in extraordinary wisdom

Among the martial artists (*bujin*) of Ryūkyū was Tokashiki *Pēchin*, a person rich in extraordinary wisdom and loved by the people as a wise man. He was born in Shuri Sakiyama and was referred to as "the Sorori Shinzaemon [56] of Ryūkyū." Besides, he also had the reputation of being a heavy drinker.

---

[56] Sorori Shinzaemon 曽呂利新左衛門, a professional comic (*rakugo*) storyteller of the 16th century. Served as a close associate of Toyotomi Hideyoshi (1536/37-1598). Originally, Sorori produced sword scabbards in Sakai. Besides being considered the founder of *rakugo*, he

One day he was dispatched to Satsuma as a government official on a ship. It seems that his martial bravery had already become known in Satsuma at that time. Challenged to a fight with a Satsuma *samurai* in the presence of the feudal lord (*daimyō*) of Satsuma, he reluctantly agreed, out of necessity. And, excelling in extraordinary wisdom, as a condition for the challenge fight, he proposed to fight upon the rush mat in the long corridor. This was approved, and so he faced Satsuma's greatest *samurai* at that time. They both confronted each other without providing the tiniest gap in their defenses. At one point, the opponent attacked shouting "Eitt!", but Tokashiki nimbly sidestepped (out of the line of attack) and quickly pulled one end of the rush mat. His opponent was thrown down, conquered, and utterly defeated. For this, Tokashiki received a word of praise by the feudal lord (*daimyō*) Shimazu of Satsuma.

Moreover, in Satsuma at that time, yet only during a specified period and at specific locations, *samurai* had the right to kill commoners for perceived affronts (*kirisute gomen*). Tokashiki intentionally violated the ban on a closed road and reached that particular location (where *kirisute gomen* was permitted), where he molested the Satsuma *samurai* by swinging his six-foot staff (*rokushaku bō*). Moreover, at that time, he fought four or five young *samurai* and utterly defeated them. He took a pledge from the young *samurai* to never again make use

---

was also a master of the tea ceremony and familiar with *waka* poems and traditional incense-smelling ceremony. His birth and death dates are unknown, but according to various theories he probably died 1597, 1603, or 1642.

of their right to kill commoners for perceived affronts. Like this, as if glowing with self-satisfaction, this is an auspicious story about a warrior (*bujin*) who went against the evil system of that time, and it seems he was considered a rarely pleasant Ryūkyūan.

Tomigusuku Satonushi, who won the countryside sumō wrestling tournament

Admired as a master of the *Koi-ryū*[57] (a school of horsemanship), Tomigusuku *Uēkata*[58] was also known as a master of the spear already in his younger days. There is also an impressive story when he quelled a countryside *sumō* wrestling tournament.

It took place when he was just twenty-four years old. One summer day, he mounted his favorite horse and went on a long ride to Katsuren and Haebaru. At that time a countryside *sumō* tournament took place at a horse-riding ground. Because of one brute fellow among them, the others alternated and replaced one another, but all were trounced (decimated), and some of them he made eat sand from the wrestling ring. Because of that, all the young men had a hard time. Seeing this, Tomigusuku, in his pronounced natural chivalry, became angry about the young man's behavior. At once, he dismounted his horse, threw off his *kimono* and

---

[57] *Koi-ryū* コイ流 and ゴイ流: Both are used in the book. For consistency, I used *Koi-ryū*.

[58] The header says Tomigusuku *Satonushi* 豊見城里之子, but the text says Tomigusuku *Uēkata*.

hakama, and *sumō*-wrestled the triumphant young man. Successfully throwing him down in the wrestling ring, Tomigusuku made him eat as much sand as possible in his mouth.

Itoman Magī, master of the secret staff (*bō*)

There is also an exciting episode about Itoman *Magī*, an unspoiled fellow of the early modern times particularly known as a master of the *bō*, rather than as a *bujin* per se.

He was born in Itoman about one hundred fifty years ago from today. Nicknamed *Ichi no Mī-gwā no Magī*[59] (*Magī* from the front of the pond), the people praised his name. Originally, Itoman is known as Ryūkyū's unique fishing village. The villagers, regardless of gender, were all engaged in fishing. *Magī* disliked fishing since childhood. Instead, from morning till night, he swung a short stick[60] against[61] the children from the neighboring houses and very much exhibited the character of a little rascal. Later, he grew up to become a strong man with a body height of 185 cm and weighing more than 120 kg. The mischief (of using a *bō*) since a very young age was helpful, and by the time he was around twenty years old, he had become known to everyone (in the martial arts circles) as a distinguished *bō*

---

[59] *Ike no Mae-gwa no Magī* 池の前小のマギー
[60] *bō-kire* 棒切: stick; piece of wood; billet; piece of a broken pole.
[61] Against, or with the children.

master. Especially when it comes to *sumō*,[62] he is said to have been unsurpassed in history. In the *sumō* circles of Ryūkyū, he substantially surpassed others and significantly distinguished himself so much that he remained unequaled ever since his time one hundred fifty years ago. From among the strong *sumō* wrestlers of the early modern period, if you look for a *sumō* wrestler who comes close to *Magī*'s reputation, I think that only Komesu of Īhu no Hama[63] in Nishihara Village comes close to him. This reminds me of an episode from those days that should prove his true value. It was when Tomigusuku *Uēkata* of Shuri and Sakiyama of Naha visited him together to test his skills. When Sakiyama challenged him to a contest with the *bō*, *Magī* frowned suspiciously, and flatly refused, saying:

> "Excuse me for being rude, but, judging from your outward appearance, you are still young at age. To fight against me is absurd. Besides, (the splendid technique of) my *bō* is not well known in public, but because I have struggled much more than anybody else in my specialty (of the *bō*) than in *sumō* wrestling, I think of myself as a distinguished expert of the *bō*. Moreover, in terms of weight, it is not just a difference of 6 to 12 kg between us, but we

[62] It is unknown what term was used at that time in Okinawa. Later Okinawa *sumō* came to be known as *shima* 角力. It starts from a position in which both contestants grips the belt of the opponent. To win, one must throw the opponent to the ground, and his back must be on the ground.

[63] Ibo no Hama 伊保之浜 was one of several villages of Nishihara which were confiscated by the US armed forces to become Nishihara Airfield following 1945.

> are separated by 48 to 54 kg. There's no way you can become my opponent!"
>
> "You should return home and practice the martial arts more earnestly, for the future. Since time immemorial, there was the aphorism called 'what vocal volume is for the singer, is physical strength/ability for the warrior.' Accordingly, you should strive to practice hard, and I hope you will become Ryūkyū's most marvelous young warrior. I'm not saying bad things. You should not become an opponent of an old man like me… Also, even if we'd become opponents and fight, there is no honor in it for you whatsoever. Quite on the contrary, it would damage the honor you have achieved until today..."

However, because it was difficult to refuse Sakiyama's request, *Magī* faced him, but after one or two bouts, he burst into great laughter, saying:

> "As I told you before, and while it might be rude, but your ability has a long way to go before it equals mine. Notwithstanding, if you keep training yourself in the martial arts, I'm looking forward to seeing you again in the future."

Like that, *Magī* tried not to further fight with Sakiyama. The weight difference between *Magī* and Tomigusuku was about 36 kg, and between *Magī* and Sakiyama it was about 54 kg, so for *Magī*, this (challenge) was entirely out of the question. Even brave Tomigusuku *Uēkata* was stunned, and, after praising *Magi*'s skills, they both hastened back to Shuri. This is a rare and funny anecdote.

Author's short curriculum vitae

VENERABLE ELDER MOTOBU Chōki's childhood name was Sanrā, and he assumed the nickname *Sārū* (monkey). He was born on April 5, 1870, as the third son of Motobu *Aji* in Shuri Akahira, Okinawa.

Having a liking for martial arts from a young age, since the age of twelve years, together with his older brother Chōyū, he formally practiced *karate* with the venerable Itosu, who visited their home. As he grew up, he furthermore studied under the two venerable gentlemen Sakuma and Matsumura. As regards *kumite*, which he studied a great deal of, besides from the above three persons, he also visited Matsumora and other martial artists (*bujin*), who were all famous in this field of expertise at that time, and asked them for instruction, or otherwise put fighting into actual practice, and he devoted himself entirely to this field of research. At that time, he had no thoughts other than

> "Martial art is me, and I am martial arts."[64]

Therefore, this kind of practice cannot possibly be attempted by ordinary people. Despite it being mid-winter, he did not make use of bedding, and if he felt cold, he got up and practiced *kata*, which warmed him up so he could go to bed. Or, when he had any doubts

[64] *Bu kore ware, ware kore bu* 武是れ我れ、我れ是れ武

about *kumite*, he almost forgot eating and sleeping over thorough consideration to figure out the best possible method, and when he realized it, he would immediately visit one of his instructors to try it out in actual practice. No matter how tough or painful it was, it is said that Motobu Chōki never neglected practice.

Indeed, by the time he was twenty-four or twenty-five, he was already a famed martial artist. Speaking of *Sārū*, no one (in Okinawa) didn't know who he was, and (in the face of his *karate* skills) everyone flinched and acknowledged his superiority. He is now at an old age. Nevertheless, he is still hale and hearty and educates the youth.

After all, even though we became close friends only very recently, I can't help but feel more and more respect and affection for his personality, which is modest, and loyal to status and honor (unattached and free from desires). As regards his skill level, people already know very well about it, so there is no need to be redundant here.

Kanna Chōjō

Impressum

Printed: March 10, 1932

Publication: March 17, 1932

Author: Motobu Chōki

Tōkyō City, Hongō ward, Dai-machi Number 2

Printer and publisher: Kanna Chōjō

Tōkyō City, Kanda ward, Omote-Sarugaku-machi 19

Printing office: Fujimoto Insatsujo

Tōkyō City, Hongō ward, Dai-machi Number 2

Publishing house: Tōkyō Karate Fukyūkai

Editor’s Addendum

Congratulatory address

Sōke of the Nihon Denryū Heihō Motobu Kenpō

President of the Nihon Karate-dō Motobu-kai

Motobu Chōsei

I am very pleased to hear that Andreas Quast *Sensei* of Germany, along with my second son, Naoki, are translating my father Motobu Chōki's *Watashi no Karate-jutsu* (*My Art and Skill of Karate*) into English. This book was my father's second book, published in 1932.

My father first published *Okinawa Kenpō Karate-jutsu Kumite-hen*, a book that mainly introduces the techniques of *kumite*, but *Watashi no Karate-jutsu* introduces photos of the *kata* Naihanchi Shodan, which was my father's specialty. In addition, *kumite* is also introduced, which includes techniques thought to be a way of dealing with *jūdō* practitioners.

At that time, my father taught *karate* on the Japanese mainland, but he had an (technical) exchange with *jūdō* practitioners, and some of those who had become his disciples were also experienced in *jūdō* and *jūjutsu.* My father was a person always brimming with curiosity, so I think that by interacting with such people, he was trying to figure out how to use *karate* to deal with it.

Besides, I think the parts elucidating the history of *karate* are also of great interest in this day and age. When I was a child, often people from Okinawa who lived in the neighborhood visited my father and had various *karate* discussions with him. Since I listened to the stories while playing on my father's side at that time, I remember some of the stories told in this book even now.

My father was genuinely interested not only in the skills of *karate* but also in its history as well as in the anecdotes about the masters in the past. Through this translation, I hope you will be able to understand one side of my father.

This summer, the Olympics will be held in Tōkyō, and *karate* will also be carried out as an official event. I think that interest in *karate* will increase through the Olympics. At the same time, I also hope that this book will promote interest in the time-honored *karate* of Okinawa.

January 25, 2020

About this publication

SALT is part of the soup, and heroic tales are part of *karate*. All schools of *karate* have their heroic stories, which establish tradition, lineage, personal relations, technical background, philosophy, moral guidelines and the like. Heroic tales also differentiate one school from others and highlight one's relative importance.

While referring to older writings and traditions, the overwhelming part of *karate*'s heroic tales – or its narratives – were created in moderns times, i.e., since the 2nd half of the 20th century. These narratives are attempts to interpret the information available at the time, for instance, the writings, oral traditions, and techniques handed down by a founder. Some sources are indispensable for the study of Okinawa *karate* and its transformation process over time. Among these, the books published by Mabuni Kenwa and Funakoshi Gichin are the most well-known and important ones.

There is, however, one primary source that has been unavailable and forgotten until rather recently: *My Art and Skill of Karate* (*Watashi no Karatejutsu*) by Motobu Chōki. This book contains the authentic experience, firsthand information, and original eye-witness accounts imparted by Motobu Chōki, one of the most knowledgable personalities in the realm of old-style Okinawa *karate*.

While this book had been printed already in 1932, its existence remained unknown until the 1980s. At that time, the wife of a deceased student of Motobu Chōki sent the book to his son, Motobu Chōsei. This one copy is the only original edition known to exist. According to the publication info page in the book, it was printed on March 10, 1932, with the official publication date scheduled for March 17, 1932. A handwritten dedication inside the book points between those two dates: On March 15, 1932, a student received the book as a gift to commemorate his promotion to 2nd-degree black belt.

So far, it is unknown how many copies were printed and what exactly happened to them. It is a fact, though, that no second copy has been verified to exist so far.

Motobu Chōsei produced some private facsimile reproductions of the solitary edition and sent the original back to its owner. At that time, in the 1980s, the book was still unknown to the general public.

It was only in 1993 when Motobu Chōsei and the *Nihon Karate-dō Motobu-kai* published about 200 or 300 official reprints of the book,[65] many of which were given as presents to students or to libraries. Like this, more than sixty years after its original publication, *My Art and Skill of Karate* by Motobu Chōki became available to the Japanese public for the first time, albeit in a relatively small number. At that time, stories such as

---

[65] Motobu Chōki: *Nihon-den-ryū Heihō Motobu Kenpō*. Sōjinsha 1993. 本部朝基著：日本伝流兵法本部拳法。拡大復刻版。壮神社、平成5年。

about *Bushi* Nagahama were still unheard of and became known for the first time.

At some point in time, Motobu Chōsei also gave one of the 1993 editions to Iwai Kohaku (aka Tsukuo). Later, in 2000 Iwai republished the book himself.[66] At that point, it became more widely available in Japanese *karate* circles.

Western *karate* circles also had noticed the significance of this work. At first, Joe Swift sent a letter to Motobu Chōsei, showing his interest in translating it. But Patrick McCarthy also worked on it and published in 2002. While his work is a compilation of all sorts of material on Motobu Chōki, it also contains a translation of *My Art and Skill of Karate*.

In other words, the knowledge, firsthand information, and original accounts imparted by Motobu Chōki in 1932 came to be known in Japan only sixty years and in the west only seventy years after its original publication.

Moreover, the postwar theories and narratives of *karate* were created and propagated without knowing the information provided by Motobu Chōki. Or in other words, Motobu Chōki's *My Art and Skill of Karate* is a rare and certainly one of the most exciting sources to assess and to interpret original old-style Okinawa *karate*.

---

[66] Iwai Kohaku: *Motobu Chōki to Ryūkyū Karate*. Tōkyō, Airyūdō 2000. 岩井虎伯：本部朝基と琉球カラテ。愛隆堂、2001。Iwai is not a student of Motobu Chōsei, but his teacher was a student of Higaonna Kamesuke. Iwai was and still is a member of the *Nihon Karate-dō Motobu-kai*.

I want to express my sincerest gratitude to Motobu Naoki, *Shihan* of the *Motobu-ryū* and grandson of Chōki. First of all, he provided me with a copy of the original 1932 edition, which was the spark that made this translation possible in the first place. The copy allowed me to reproduce the old photos in the best possible quality. Moreover, without his unreserved advice, explanation, and translation and his unfettered and sustained readiness to fully support this project at any point during the long period of its formation, the translation of this excellent work wouldn't have become a reality.

I would also like to express my sincerest gratitude to Motobu Chōsei *Sensei* (*1925), son of Chōki and *Sōke* of the *Motobu-ryū*, for ennobling this publication with his congratulatory address (see page 185).

January 2020

Andreas Quast

On divine speed

Yabu Kentsū was a long-time partner of Motobu Chōki. And both were fellow students of Matsumura Sōkon. As Motobu noted, it was important in those days to choose a good partner for *kumite*:

> "Those who attempt to practice *kumite* should always choose opponents suitable to them, and who understand that in *kumite* **agility and speed** is the most important thing."

After all, Motobu Chōki's *kumite* drills should include original ideas of Matsumura Sōkon, a hint to which we find in the expression "warriors value divine speed."[67] Motobu emphasized this concept as the most important thing in *kumite*.

Well, this expression is generally interpreted to explain the importance of the physical speed of a thrust in *karate*. Indeed, this is not wrong and fits *karate* as a martial art. It also might refer to one's overall agility, or to the speed of one's reaction time, both in distant as well as in tactile situations. There are many possibilities.

Anyway, just as Matsumura's reference to the *7 Virtues of Martial Arts* was a reference to an ancient

---

[67] *bushi ha shinsoku o tattobu* 武士は神速を尊ぶ. This is according to the autobiography of Yoshimura Chōgi, likewise a student of Matsumura.

Chinese text,[68] so is his expression "warriors value divine speed."

The ancient Chinese source is the expression *bing gui shen su* 兵貴神速. It is found in the *Legend of Guo Jia* within the *Sanguozhi* (History of the Three Kingdoms). This expression translates to "soldiers value great speed." Figuratively it means to do something swift and resolute, and that speed is a crucial asset in war. In Japanese, the phrase transcribes to *hei ha shinsoku o tattobu* 兵は神速を尊ぶ. It is the same as in Matsumura's case, only soldier (*hei* 兵) has been replaced with martial artist (*bushi* 武士).

The story behind it is as follows: Guo Jia (170-207) served as a strategist of statesman and general Cao Cao (155-220). In 207, Cao Cao advanced to Yijing during on a punitive expedition against the proto-Mongolic Wuhuan people. At the Battle of White Wolf Mountain, Guo Jia advised Cao Cao,

> "Soldiers value great speed. Leave behind the heavy military equipment and let only the light cavalry advance forward day and night. Let's take the enemy by surprise!"

In short: the expression explains the importance of surprise attacks in battle and of preventing long, exhausting campaigns. Once it is inevitable, it is better to act swiftly, take the enemy by surprise, and settle the

[68] See: Quast, Andreas: King Wu Once Buckled On His Armor: The Seven Virtues of Martial Arts. Ryukyu Bugei, Band 1. 2016.

matter in a short time while protecting valuable resources.

What does it mean for *karate*? In Motobu's words, it means "*karate* is to attack first," or "you don't need to defend every weak attack by your opponent. Instead, you should attack yourself without pausing."

Matsumura was familiar with the art of war. This can be understood by reading the letter addressed to his disciple Kuwae Ryōsei. [69] Therefore, the expression "warriors value great speed" emphasizes the importance of making the first move, to seize the initiative, to forestall. This seems to be the meaning of *sente* 先手 as Motobu understood it. Besides, "divine speed" might also include the meaning of conserving valuable resources, that is, to act economically.

---

[69] See: Quast, Andreas: King Wu Once Buckled On His Armor: The Seven Virtues of Martial Arts. Ryukyu Bugei, Band 1. 2016.

Notes on personalities

- Tomigusuku *Uēkata* (see page 173): This person is considered to be Tomigusuku *Uēkata* Seiko (1829-1893, 豊見城親方盛綱). Tomigusuku was a student of Sakiyama, who in turn was a student of Chinese military officer Ason:

> "The majority of people received their initiation [into empty-handed martial art] directly from a Chinese in China or in our prefecture. **Students of Ason are Sakiyama from Izumizaki (the teacher of Tomigusuku *Uēkata*)**, Nagahama, Tomoyose and Gushi Pēchin (the teacher of Ishimine from Gibo)."[70]

- Tomigusuku *Uēkata*'s chestnut-colored horse is described as having been 182 cm tall (see page 160). This height most probably did not refer to the withers, but the height of the head instead.

- In the chronological chart (see page 165) at the end of the original text, Ginowan *Dunchi* and Morishima *Uēkata* are presented as two

[70] From: Okinawa no Bugi (Ryūkyū Shinpō, January 1914) written by Shōtō (Funakoshi Gichin).

different persons. However, this is a mistake, and both names are the same person. After detailed consideration of the text, the chronology, and the eras, there is little doubt that this position was originally intended for Makabe *Chān*. Both were corrected in this translation.

- Ginowan *Dunchi* was shortened to Giwan *Dunchi* in the text, but this is not correct. His original name was Ginowan. Only at the time of Ginowan *Dunchi*'s son Chōho, the name was changed to Giwan. The reason was that a member of the royal family had been named Ginowan at that time, but no other person was allowed to bear the current name of a member of the royal family.

- Sakugawa's 'triangle jump' (*sankaku tobi*, see page 154) might be something similar to the jumping feats of Jacky Chan and his likes, or what can be seen at a show-jumping course (Parcours). That is, according to the description, it seems Sakugawa jumped against one wall at a corner – hence 'triangular walls' – and from there pushed (=kicked) himself off to the other wall.

- *Tsuken Hanta-gwā* 津堅ハンタ小 (see pages 152, 154, and 165): Tsuken is a smaller island located at the Pacific Ocean side of Okinawa

Main Island, at Uruma City. *Hanta-gwā* is written in *katakana* as ハンタ小, but the characters for this word are 端小. It means edge, point, border, or cape. For example, the border of a village, or the edge of a cliff, and also the cliff itself. In general, it refers to sharply broken terrain. The person nicknamed Tsuken *Hanta-gwā* was described as a 'master of the *bō*.' There is a technique called '*gyakute hanta-gwā*' found in a few *kata* of Okinawan *bōjutsu*.

- *Shichiyanaka Usumē* 下中爺 (see pages 152, 154, and 166) was also mentioned as a master of the *bō*. His *bōjutsu* has had been handed down under the name of *Chinen Shikiyanaka no Kon*. Moreover, there is also *Sakugawa no Kon*, *Chatan Yara no Kon*, and *Tawada no Sai*. The latter, Tawada, had been described as a student of Matsumura who was on a par with Itosu and Asato. Tawada appears to have been a bit stronger than Asato (Yoshimura Chōgi, 1941). Motobi Chōki mentioned all the above persons. And all these *kata* contain characteristic techniques of *Ryūkyū Bugei*.
- *Ōta Nagasutarū* 太田長小樽 (see pages 152, 156, and 165) – The younger brother of Ōta *Aji*. According to Yoshimura Chōgi (1941), *there was a powerful person named Nagasutarū from the Goeku Udun*. It's true; a son of the Goeku Udun used the title of 'Ōta Aji.' While this needs more research, if it turns out to be accurate,

than this would elucidate new details of Ōta *Aji* and Ōta Nagasutarū, of the Goeku *Udun*, and of the *Ryūkyū Bugei.*

- *Itarashiki* 板良敷 (see page 161), alias *Akāyamā* アカー山 – This person is Itarashiki Chōiku 板良敷朝郁, a famous singer. His name was mentioned in the same breath with Arakaki Ankichi, Kyan Chōtoku, and Motobu Chōki, the latter of which clearly respected Itarashiki for his *karate* skills and as an elder.

- *Makiya* 眞喜屋 (see page 160) – Described only in passing as someone who had disciples in horsemanship. Yoshimura Chōgi reported that he himself studied with a famous cavalry captain named Makiya between around 1885–89. Looking back further in history, during official Ryūkyūan missions to the *Shōgun* in Edo, in the years 1710, 1714, 1748, and 1764, a member of the Makiya clan served as the chief horseman of the mission. In Edo, this Makiya Pēchin was also among the smaller group who proceeded to the Shōgun's castle for the audience (This all is found recorded in the *Tsūkō Ichiran, Ryūkyū Kunibu* Vol. 9–14). Obviously, the Makiya served as horsemen in Ryūkyū for quite an extended period. There is also a book about the Makiya clan's horsemanship in existence. There can be little doubt that the Makiya mentioned by Motobu

Chōki was from the same old family of horsemen. Actually, and this is rarely discussed, some *shihanke* 師範家 (instructor) families appear to have lived in Ryūkyū. And the Makiya family was a *shihanke* of horsemanship.

- Matsumura 松村, Yabu Kentsū 屋部憲通, and 'kicking upward' (*keri-age* 蹴上げ, see page 157) – Yabu Kentsū and Motobu Chōki were good friends and had also practiced together. Before World War II, Motobu Chōki told his son Motobu Chōsei the following about Yabu Kentsū: "Yabu, standing with his back to the wall, kicked upward so that his toes reached the wall behind him. That's a great feat!" In other words, Yabu was able to kick up and behind him. In Motobu Chōki's school, as a general rule, no kicks higher than belt level are performed. So while they were fellows, and even both trained under Matsumura, they seem to have had different ideas about technique anyway. However, as can be seen in the translation of Motobu Chōki's text given earlier, Matsumura obviously kicked similar to Yabu *Sensei*. In the text, Matsumura is described as being 'excellent in kicking upwards. Occasionally, when a comrade tried to restrain him by throwing his arms around him from behind, although Matsumura *Sensei* could not use his hands, he freely kicked up with his legs on the left and the right. In this way, he kicked down the person…' In other words,

Matsumura and Yabu both used this kicking technique.

Notes on terminology

- *bujin* 武人 – In his text, Motobu Chōki frequently used the term *bujin* 武人. In Japanese *bujin* refers to a warrior, soldier, and military man. However, for the historical context of Ryūkyū and for this article these translations are improper for various reasons, a detailed explanation of which is beyond the given scope. In any case, in this text, the term 'martial artist' was consistently used as a translation of *bujin*.

- *karate* 唐手 – Throughout the original text, the characters *karate* 唐手 appears. The *furigana* added as a reading aid leaves no doubt: it is without exception pronounced *karate*, not *tōdī*. Moreover, some words were written in a mix of Japanese and Uchināguchi. It may be assumed that a reason for this was that the book was published in Tōkyō, mainland Japan, and for Japanese customers to read. As a result, the text says '*Karate* Sakugawa' instead of '*Tōdī* Sakugawa.' However, *karate* 唐手 is something utterly different from *tōdī* 唐手. Therefore, in the instances were Sakugawa is mentioned with his nickname, it was transcribed correctly here as '*Tōdī* Sakugawa.'

- *tsukite* (Oki.: *chichidi*) 突き手 – This intriguing expression appears seven times in the text. On the one hand, it is used in the phrase 'master of *tsukite*' (*tsukite no meijin* 突き手の名人). On the other hand, it is used in variations of the expression 'known as a *tsukite*' (*tsukite toshite shirareru* 突き手として知られる). From the context of the phrase within the text corpus, *tsuki* 突き solely refers to thrusting or striking with the bare parts of the human body. *Te* 手, as has become well-known these days, does not necessarily refer to 'hand' in the literal sense. Quite on the contrary: the lexical meaning also includes such translations as ways, means, method, mode, a trick or artifice, and even a hold as in catching or seizing. *Tsukite* (*chichidi*) might, therefore, simply but adequately be interpreted as an 'art of striking with bare parts of the human body.' And finally, on the one hand, it refers to the method itself, and on the other, it refers to a person who is skilled in it. That is, an expert of *karate*. This should be sufficient for now.

- *ashiwaza* 足技 – This term was used in connection with Tawada and Oyadomari. It is translated here as 'kicking technique'. However, keep in mind that it also might be interpreted as 'leg techniques', 'foot techniques', or even 'footwork'.

- *nawagiri* 縄切り – It means 'rope tearing.' According to the description, Makishi's special technique was escapology.

- *zai* 釺 – In the text, there is a weapon referred to as *zai* 釺. The *kun* reading of it is *surudoi* するどい (鋭い), which relates to something pointed or sharp. This utensil was interpreted here as being *sai* 釵. Gima the *Chikusaji* is said to have been skilled with the *sai* and since *Chikusaji* were the policemen of old Ryūkyū, and since furthermore *sai* or *bō* were their service weapons, this is the most likely option and should be maintained until proven otherwise.

- As regards the secondary villa the ferocious bull was held at (see page 157): The king had several secondary villas. One of them was the Gusukuma *Udun* 城間御殿, in today's Urasoe City. Of course, it might also have been a different place.

Index

C

D

G

H

I

O

P

R

S

U

W

Y

Z

Printed in Great Britain
by Amazon

36384071R00139